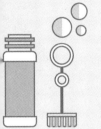

ADVENTURES IN AUTHENTIC LEARNING

21 Step-by-Step Projects From an Edtech Coach

Kristin Harrington

International Society for Technology in Education

PORTLAND, OREGON ✦ ARLINGTON, VIRGINIA

Adventures in Authentic Learning

21 Step-by-Step Projects From an Edtech Coach

Kristin Harrington

© 2020 International Society for Technology in Education

Senior Director of Books and Journals: *Colin Murcray*

Senior Acquisitions Editor: *Valerie Witte*

Development and Copyeditor: *Linda Laflamme*

Proofreader: *Joanna Szabo*

Indexer: *Valerie Haynes Perry*

Book Design and Production: *Danielle Foster*

Cover Design: *Beth DeWilde*

Library of Congress Cataloging-in-Publication Data Available

First Edition

ISBN: 978-1-56484-881-9

Ebook version available

Printed in the United States of America

ISTE® is a registered trademark of the International Society for Technology in Education.

Dedication

This book is dedicated to all the educators and students I have been so fortunate to work with and learn from. You inspired the ideas in this book and continue pushing me to be better every day.

ABOUT ISTE

The *International Society for Technology in Education* (ISTE) is a nonprofit organization that works with the global education community to accelerate the use of technology to solve tough problems and inspire innovation. Our worldwide network believes in the potential technology holds to transform teaching and learning.

ISTE sets a bold vision for education transformation through the ISTE Standards, a framework for students, educators, administrators, coaches and computer science educators to rethink education and create innovative learning environments. ISTE hosts the annual ISTE Conference & Expo, one of the world's most influential edtech events. The organization's professional learning offerings include online courses, professional networks, year-round academies, peer-reviewed journals and other publications. ISTE is also the leading publisher of books focused on technology in education. For more information or to become an ISTE member, visit **iste.org**. Subscribe to ISTE's YouTube channel and connect with ISTE on Twitter, Facebook and LinkedIn.

Related ISTE Titles

Reinventing Project-Based Learning: Your Field Guide to Real-World Projects in the Digital Age, Third Edition
Suzie Boss and Jane Krauss

Inspiring Curiosity: The Librarian's Guide to Inquiry-Based Learning
Colette Cassinelli

To see all books available from ISTE, please visit iste.org/books.

ABOUT THE AUTHOR

 Kristin Harrington is an edtech coach for Flagler County School District in Palm Coast, FL, as well as an adjunct professor for Flagler College in St. Augustine, FL. She has a master's degree in Educational Technology and Instructional Design from the University of Florida. Kristin is the president of the ISTE Learning Spaces Network, a guest writer for ISTE's *Empowered Learner Magazine* and blog, and a recipient of the 2020 ISTE Edtech Coaches Award. She is also the co-founder of Edcamp St. Augustine and Edcamp Flagler, as well as the secretary of the Florida Council of Instructional Technology Leaders (FCITL).

As an educator Kristin worked in both private and public schools, before transitioning into her current role as a coach.

Acknowledgments

Thanks to everyone on the ISTE publishing team for your tremendous help and support with writing my first book. To my editors Valerie Witte and Linda Laflamme, I truly couldn't have done this without your help, and I appreciate all of your kind and thoughtful feedback throughout this process. This was truly a team effort, and this is a much better book because of your help and support.

To my family, thank you for believing in me even when I may not have always earned it. To my friends, thank you for listening to me talk about this book for the past two years and for never complaining. Aren't you glad it's finished? To my favorite people, Brady and Nate, may you always have your love of learning and creativity. You all have inspired me more than you know!

Publisher's Acknowledgments

Manuscript Reviewers:
Rich Dixon
Sheryl O'Shea
Shaundel Krumheuer
Chip Cash

ISTE Standards Reviewers:
Donna Albertson
Carolina Seiden
Kim Lowden
Aimee Bloom

CONTENTS

CHAPTER 3

COLLABORATE FOR SUCCESS   73

CHAPTER 4

DESIGNING MEANINGFUL PROJECTS   111

INTRODUCTION

Seeing the excitement on a student's face when they create, solve, or accomplish something new is an amazing and contagious experience. For many educators, this is why we teach, and this feeling inspires us to continue searching for new ways to achieve this and seek new adventures in our classrooms. Student enthusiasm for learning can happen at any grade level, although it's arguably more difficult to achieve in middle- and high-school classrooms. In my role as an edtech coach, I continually work to create these experiences for both students and teachers. I have found that more often than not, this enthusiasm happens in conjunction with authentic projects. The ISTE Standards for Students (International Society for Technology in Education [ISTE], 2016) recognize this as well, calling on teachers to encourage communication, creativity, student voice and choice, and other important skills to help develop engaged and lifelong learners.

As an edtech coach, I have the unique opportunity to truly see what is happening in the classrooms where I work, as well as gather a wealth of ideas from the teachers I coach. Through collaboration, shared ideas can build into something great that needs to be shared with an even broader group. That's partly how *Adventures in Authentic Learning* came about: Many of the projects and insights I share in this book grew from reflecting on classroom collaborations—between coach and teacher, teacher and students, and students and their peers. So whether you are a teacher or edtech coach, or fill another role in our schools, my hope is that you will take ideas from this book and build upon them, making them even better.

Many of the ideas and projects in this book focus on a similar goal: to foster communication skills and empower students as they engage in learning experiences that are authentic. So what does this mean? To me, authentic lessons incorporate some element of student choice and topics relevant to students. They also involve students in solving a problem or creating something, while engaging in tasks that incorporate skills we typically see in the workforce and our world outside of school. The ISTE Standards for Students focus on helping students build these much-needed skills, making them the perfect blueprint for getting started with helping your students become lifelong empowered learners and competent and creative communicators. To help you implement these standards with your students, as well as fulfill the ISTE Standards for Educators (ISTE, 2017), you'll find numerous connections between the standards and the project ideas presented in this book.

Throughout *Adventures in Authentic Learning*, you'll find suggestions and tools to help you engage students in authentic projects as well as research-rooted answers to questions I commonly receive from the teachers I coach. Each chapter contains a "Lesson Plans" section featuring step-by-step lessons and project documents you can immediately implement with your students—whether in the classroom or in a remote-learning environment.

Look for the and icons to see which portions of a project are best implemented face-to-face and which ones students can accomplish working online, either independently or collaboratively.

Additionally, each chapter ends with a "Coach's Connection" section to assist educational technology coaches who are collaborating with teachers to implement authentic projects. Each "Coach's Connection" section features strategies and tips that align with the ISTE Standards for Coaches (ISTE, 2019), providing strategies and ideas to help you collaborate with teachers and better support students when implementing authentic learning lessons. Although these sections were designed for coaches, they contain useful information for any educator.

In addition, each chapter contains strategies and resources to help you engage in authentic projects. You'll learn about developing a project mindset, time management, creating projects with an authentic purpose, and helping students become better presenters. Resource links are provided throughout the book, and Appendix C serves as the *Adventures in Authentic Learning* toolbox, listing all the recommended resources and templates in one place.

As you read, I hope you share the enthusiasm I felt as I wrote this book. I am often amazed by how teachers take my suggestions even further with ideas I would never have thought of myself. Similarly, in the classroom, my most memorable and enjoyable times were when students were exploring, creating, and making their own meaning through research projects, book trailers, engineering challenges, and other authentic learning opportunities.

The satisfaction of witnessing students move beyond our expectations is immense. There is little more rewarding than hearing about students going home and working tirelessly on a project because they are so engaged and invested in the outcome. As the school year progresses and students become more comfortable with authentic, project-based learning, you will see them grow in their mastery of collaborating, speaking on-camera, writing, and other skills that will benefit them beyond the classroom. Simply put, authentic learning adventures are fun—not just for your students, but for you as well. So whether you are stuck in a rut filled with workbooks and test prep or just need some fresh ideas for your already engaging classroom, this book will provide ideas and projects so you can have fun working with your students and get excited for each new day as an educator.

CHAPTER 1

FOCUS ON THE LEARNING, NOT THE PRODUCT

Early in my teaching career, I realized the power of beginning with the end in mind. My first attempt at a weather lesson that gave students the opportunity to become weather forecasters highlighted this especially (see Lesson Plan 1.1). I showed them a forecast from our local news, as well as a student example, and they were hooked by the video of a student standing in front of a tornado pretending to be blown away.

I felt encouraged by their initial enthusiasm for the project, but I truly understood how valuable my introduction had been when I started delivering the weather content. While the class watched a BrainPOP video about natural disasters, students started exclaiming, "Pause it! Pause it," and then furiously writing notes. I realized then that their "need to know" was so much deeper than getting a good grade. They wanted to write a realistic script and create the best weather forecast video they could. This behavior continued throughout the unit.

I must confess that the first year we tried the project, many of my students did not finish their weather forecast videos due to a string of unfortunate events. Most notably, the yellow rain ponchos students wore interfered with the green screen enough that students looked like ghosts or holograms. They thought it was hilarious, but all I could think of was the time wasted and that we would need to reshoot everything. I considered the project a disaster and vowed to ban yellow rain ponchos from my classroom! In hindsight, however, I understand that the important aspect of this project was the learning that took place and how engaged students were in the process because they knew they would be able to apply their knowledge in a meaningful way. Although these types of projects take longer than we usually anticipate, I believe they will be what students remember when they look back on their education years.

Let's face it: Projects get messy, and sometimes they do not get finished. This can be frustrating and discouraging, possibly leading us to believe that projects are not "our thing" or will not work with "this class" or "this grade level." When you focus on the process more than the final product, however, you'll begin to see that the messiness is often when the best learning happens. This chapter focuses on getting you into that positive mindset to begin projects in your classroom. We will discuss how to frame projects for success, as well as how to truly assess what students are learning along the way. In addition, I provide some ideas for how you can use the ISTE Standards for Students, and in particular the Empowered Learner standard, to help students create their own yearlong, project-based goals, as well as assess their own learning.

Developing a Project Mindset

One way to ensure that you remain in a positive project mindset and focus on the process is by engaging in regular check-ins to gauge not only your students' progress with the project but also their level of understanding with the concepts you are teaching. This is easier to do when you think of the project as the main course, rather than the dessert. Students typically complete projects at the end of a unit to demonstrate what they've learned, like dessert at the end of a meal. Instead, I encourage you to weave the project throughout your unit, helping you and your students focus on the process. Here is an example of how this might look:

+ Lesson Introduction. Grab your students' attention with a video, experiment, or other engaging content. Provide students with the rubric and project description. This is also a good time to assess students' prior knowledge and interest in the topic.

+ Vocabulary Instruction Mini-Lesson. Many of my project rubrics focus on students using vocabulary in context. Early in your unit, I recommend incorporating content vocabulary with graphic organizers, such as Frayer Models, and opportunities for students to practice writing and speaking with content words.

+ Content Introduction. At this point in your project, students are still engaging at Bloom's Taxonomy levels 1 and 2, working to recall and develop a basic understanding of the content. This is a good time to use videos, articles, textbook content, and class discussion mini-lessons. As students move further into the project, they will be practicing Bloom's Taxonomy levels 3 through 6, so establishing this foundation will ensure that they are able to engage at a deeper level. Make sure students begin taking notes to help them when developing their project later.

+ Project Time. Divide students into groups and allow them to begin brainstorming topics and ideas for their projects.

+ Content Mini-Lesson. Review previous content and provide students with opportunities to begin applying their knowledge in small ways. For example, in the Weather Forecast Project (Lesson Plan 1.1), students can apply their knowledge of the water cycle by conducting an experiment and making a hypothesis about what will happen. Students can later apply this knowledge in their weather forecast videos, predicting how long flooding will last and describing what happens to water after a flood.

+ Project Time. Give students time to begin developing their projects.

+ Mini-Lesson. Once students have started their projects is a great time for teachable moments. Did you observe any misconceptions as students created their scripts, plans, and so on? Did you notice grammatical errors or difficulties with locating valid sources? Add "Just in Time" lessons here to help students get what they need to design a quality project.

This cycle of project time and mini-lessons can continue, as you adapt to meet the needs of your students and each individual project. Once you begin to adapt your lessons to incorporate projects throughout your unit, you will be surprised at how quickly this becomes second nature to you.

Goal Setting for Empowerment

I like to think of the Empowered Learner standard as foundational, and that the other ISTE Standards for Students build on it. This standard encourages students to take ownership of their learning by setting their own goals, choosing collaborators and technology tools, and reflecting on the process of their learning (ISTE Standards for Students, 1a, 2016). This does not happen overnight but is powerful to watch as students transform from passengers to drivers who feel in control and have a say in what they learn and how.

One thing that will help this transformation is to provide students with opportunities to set goals for their learning, or as the Facilitator standard states, to "foster a culture where students take ownership of their learning goals and outcomes in both independent and group settings as guidelines" (ISTE Standards for Educators, 6a, 2017). This process will need to be heavily scaffolded at first: Provide students with sentence stems, examples, and choices to help them set achievable and effective goals. At the beginning of the year, for example, I recommend helping students create yearlong goals based on things they would like to accomplish. As the school year progresses, you can then encourage them to align unit and project goals with their overarching goals. Here are three ways to encourage students to set and monitor their goals:

✦ Goal Cubes. At the beginning of the year, have students paint wooden or 3D printed cubes, and then write or paint words or pictures on the sides to express the goals they would like to accomplish. Students keep these cubes (or dice) in their desks, cubbies, or lockers throughout the year, helping them stay focused on what they indicated is important. In my classroom, I showed a short video clip with examples of goals they could set, such as strategies for being a good friend, reading books from various genres, or completing timed fact fluency problems in two minutes. I allowed students to set extracurricular goals as well, as long as they included at least two academic goals. We talked about how goals need to be measurable and discussed that "buying a Nintendo Switch" is not an appropriate goal. Again, scaffolding is key here. To add some novelty to this activity, have students periodically roll their cubes like a die and then write, create an audio recording, or discuss how they are progressing with that particular goal.

- Idea Boards. Ask students to cut out photographs from magazines to represent their goals and create drawings on cardstock paper or cardboard. For example, if a student's goal is to earn an industry certification in Adobe Photoshop, they might include a picture of the Photoshop logo on their board. Students can then store these idea boards in a folder or data notebook, or you can display them on your classroom walls so they are easily accessible throughout the year. Another option is to save a picture of the idea board online in your learning management system (LMS), or even as wallpaper on student devices.

- Flip Boards. Create a topic board with Flipgrid (**info.flipgrid.com**) to which students can post videos and respond with video comments. For goal setting, have students brainstorm ideas for their goals and create a video to post on the class Flipgrid board. Throughout the year, students can listen to their video and post responses to reflect on their progress toward their goals. If you are not familiar with Flipgrid, it is a great tool for incorporating student voices in your classroom, and it is free.

The most important aspects of the student goal-setting process are building in time for students to revisit and reflect on their goals throughout the year and providing opportunities for them to communicate their goal progress to their teachers, parents, classmates, and themselves. To ensure that these important check-ins actually happen, build the necessary time into your lesson plans at the beginning of the year. I have observed so many creative ways to do this, such as a Donut and Data discussion, where students eat breakfast and conference with their parents to explain the progress they've made toward their goals. Donuts and Data can occur several times a year or quarterly, providing time for parents to learn more about their child's academic progress and goals. You can even involve your students in brainstorming ways they can reflect on and discuss their goals throughout the year.

Assessing Student Learning During Projects

One of the most frequent questions teachers ask me about implementing projects and cooperative learning is how to assess student learning and cooperation. Most grading policies do not allow for students to be formally assessed on soft skills, so assessments can be tricky to implement in a way that students value. Plus, when there is so much going on in the classroom simultaneously during project-based learning (PBL), how do you effectively evaluate each group? The sections that follow offer a few ideas for assessing student collaboration and ensuring that students feel their work is valued.

Create a Rubric

Create a rubric or checklist to detail your specific student expectations for a project or presentation and provide it to students prior to beginning the project unit. Rubrics help quantify these expectations, listing categories with levels of student proficiency and then assigning points for each level achieved. Not only will a rubric help alleviate any anxiety or unknowns students feel about the project, but it also acts as an anticipation guide. A well-designed rubric or checklist shows students what to pay attention to and the learning that they will need to create a successful project or presentation. You can find rubric examples in many of the lesson plans included near the end of each chapter.

If your school or district purchased a learning management system, it most likely has a built-in rubric creator. This may be the easiest way to create a rubric, as you can attach it to assignments and submit scores from the rubric directly into your LMS gradebook.

If you don't have access to an LMS but need help getting started with rubrics, check out PBLWorks (**pblworks.org**). In addition to offering a wealth of information on project-based learning, the PBLWorks website hosts various rubrics you can use for scoring projects, as well as rubrics for scoring your students' collaboration and research skills. In addition, "The Feynman Project" (Lesson Plan 4.2) contains a template for a rubric I created in Google Sheets. Google Sheets works well for rubrics because it totals the scores for you, and the documents are easy to share with students and other teachers.

No matter how you create them, rubrics are also a great way to address the Digital Citizen standard, which states, "Students recognize the rights, responsibilities and opportunities of living, learning and working in an interconnected digital world, and they act and model in ways that are safe, legal and ethical" (ISTE Standards for Students, 2016). "Copyright and Citations" can be included as its own category in a rubric, or can be incorporated with another category, such as "Project Design" or "Research." Examples of this are included in Lesson Plan 3.4, as well as Lesson Plan 4.1. Even in primary classrooms, students can begin developing an understanding of copyrights and giving credit, providing an author's name or the title of a website where they retrieved their facts or photo. In upper grades, students can learn how to format proper citations and will already have background knowledge about the importance of creator's rights.

Turn Observations into Quantitative Data

Although not meant to be a daily assessment tool, tracking student cooperative learning can provide insight into the level of engagement in collaborative groups, as well as the effectiveness of their interactions. At times, students can appear to be off-task, disruptive, or disinterested in a project, but taking a closer look will show that things are not always what they seem.

While observing cooperative learning, set a timer for two minutes to watch one group interact. It is best if you can observe from a distance, so students are not aware you are watching. While the timer counts down, watch for and tally three types of interactions (Barron, 2000):

+ Parallel. Students exchange comments during a task but with limited attempts to share ideas and monitor peers.

+ Associative. Students share information about the task but do not attempt to assign roles.

+ Cooperative. Students monitor each other, assign roles, and work together to solve problems. This is the ideal type of interaction.

This continues as you monitor each group for two minutes. You may need more than one class period to complete all the tracking sessions. In addition, you can also assess the types of positive and negative interactions (see Table 1.1) to evaluate the level of cooperative learning taking place in each group (Barron, 2000). These observations can be used in an online learning environment as well. Using a videoconference tool such as Zoom, students can work in breakout rooms while you move between rooms to complete the observations with each group.

TABLE 1.1 Types of Student Cooperative Learning Interactions

TYPE	INTERACTIONS
Positive Interactions	Acceptances: Students listen to their peers' ideas and accept their responses as valid and/or worthy ideas.
	Clarifications: Students clarify the ideas of their peers.
	Elaborations: Students build on the ideas of their peers, adding additional information.
Negative Interactions	Rejections: Students reject the ideas their peers present.
	Lack of Response: Students ignore the ideas their peers present.

After tallying the results of your students' interactions within their groups, share this valuable information with each group respectively. All of these interactions are normal and frequently observed in cooperative learning environments. By relaying this information to students, you can help them develop a better understanding of how they are interacting with their peers and better self-awareness about how they cooperate with others.

Setting a Foundation for Project Success

Projects and project-based learning often involve taking risks and learning from failed attempts (remember my ghostly rain ponchos?). To encourage them to take such risks, students need a comfortable and inclusive classroom environment, where they feel safe and supported when taking chances and working with others. Additionally, when students work in teams during cooperative projects, team members need to value differences and learn that diverse skills, cultures, and interests help strengthen project products. The following sections provide ideas to help prepare your students and classroom for cooperative projects, ensuring that everyone feels represented, valued, and heard.

Culturally Responsive Teaching

Prior to beginning the year, I recommend analyzing your book collection, room decor, and teaching materials to determine if you are promoting cultural and other types of diversity. Each student should feel represented in your classroom and school, and if they are not represented in the population of students and staff, then it is especially important to read diverse literature, as well as invite face-to-face and virtual guest speakers.

When implementing projects, you can incorporate culturally responsive and inclusive resources and practices in many ways. For example, challenge students to highlight books written by diverse authors or that include diverse characters when creating book trailers (Lesson Plan 1.3). Guest speakers are an excellent addition to projects and a great opportunity to feature professionals from diverse backgrounds. During the Weather Forecast Project, imagine the impact it would have on Black students to videoconference with a meteorologist who looks like them or for a student with a disability to interact with a successful scientist who also has a disability. (For more ideas on in-person and videoconference guest speakers, see Chapter 3.)

Class and Team Building

Building a positive culture and making students feel welcome is something that great teachers have always made a priority; however, through learning sciences research, we can now truly see the impact of these practices. According to Schwartz, Tsang, and Blair, belonging is one of our most fundamental needs, and it is essential in order for productive learning to occur (2016). This is especially true when implementing projects, as students need to feel comfortable giving and receiving feedback, expressing their ideas, and respectfully debating topics when needed. At the beginning of the year, one activity that worked well in my classroom was to conduct multiple intelligence surveys with my students. Another research-based strategy is using scripts to help students learn how to interact appropriately and effectively. Both of these activities are helpful in creating a class culture that is conducive to project-based learning.

Multiple Intelligences Surveys

In elementary school, I used Howard Gardner Multiple Intelligences assessments, which I called the "How Are We Smart?" exercise, to help students appreciate the diversity in others, as well as help me facilitate lessons that would meet the needs of all learners (Figure 1.1). Recent research has created a debate about the validity of Gardner's intelligences, but I still feel that interest surveys can help students understand themselves better and appreciate how different preferences and interests can be beneficial when working cooperatively. If you are teaching in an online classroom, you can create a form for students to indicate their responses. Both Google Forms and Microsoft Forms allow graphics to be answer choices, making your form simple for the youngest learners to complete.

1.1 You can use a multiple intelligence assessment like this one in primary grades to help students appreciate their classmates' interests and talents.

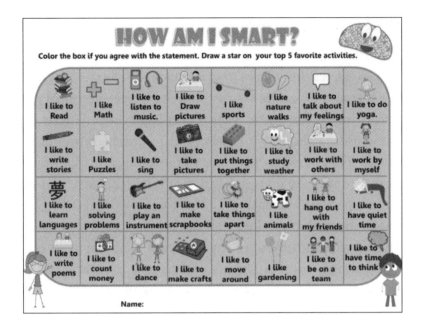

Using Scripts to Teach Social Skills

Goodyear, Jones, and Thompson demonstrated how the use of scripts can help students develop social skills and learn how to effectively work cooperatively (2014). More specifically, *social scripts* assist students in collaborating with their peers, while *epistemic scripts* help students focus on their task. In my projects, I tend to combine these two types together into one script or project guide. (You can see an example of this in Lesson 1.2.) Scripts can be as simple as providing students with sentence stems to help them get their conversation started:

+ "Let's make sure everyone has a chance to talk . . ."

+ "I would like to add to your idea by . . ."

+ "I like your idea, but have a few questions about . . ."

Scripts can help students monitor their own interactions, ask each other relevant questions, explain their thinking, and participate in healthy debates. You can also expand scripts to provide specific roles for each student. For example, Student A could be responsible for ensuring everyone gets an opportunity to share their ideas, while Student B could be tasked with listing pros and cons for each idea. Kagan Cooperative Learning's structures, such as Numbered Heads Together and Stand Up, Hand Up, Pair Up, are examples of scripts.

Initially, I was skeptical of the value of scripts. I felt like scripts might impede genuine social interactions and interfere with creativity and spontaneous moments of genius that occur when students collaborate. Over time, I began to see the benefits, particularly for younger students and students with limited social skills. For example, in a STEM engineering project I initiated with first-grade classes, I observed students working parallel to each other, rather than communicating and problem solving together. I recognized that a script would be helpful and created one to use with subsequent classes. I found that students took turns when speaking and using materials. While using the script, they asked more questions and were able to stay focused on the project. You can introduce scripts at the beginning of the year or when you first introduce projects. Then, as students learn how to collaborate more effectively, you can gradually reduce or even eliminate script use.

Short cooperative learning tasks are ideal for introducing the use of scripts. For example, during a mini-lesson to kick off a unit on biographies, ask students to work with a partner to generate a list of influential Americans and provide some script sentence stems to facilitate the project. Supplying a script to students while working in small groups to tackle a three-step math problem can help those who usually struggle with math concepts to speak up. Using scripts on a regular basis will help students develop social skills they need to participate in more complex projects later on.

LESSON PLANS

So now you have a better understanding of what it takes to prep students for participating in projects. The three lessons that follow use some of the strategies mentioned in this chapter. As you read each lesson plan, notice the context surrounding the use of rubrics, check-ins, and scripts. You might recognize some other strategies as well.

LESSON PLAN 1.1 Weather Forecast Project

Subject: Science/ELA

Target Grades: 2–5

Duration: 2–3 weeks (throughout weather unit)

Students will become junior meteorologists and create their own green-screen weather forecast videos. They will explain the weather and provide severe weather safety tips during their video.

Objectives

Grades 2 and 3 students will be able to:

+ Write a script and produce their own video.

+ List several severe weather safety tips and understand the importance of following safety rules during severe weather.

+ Use science content vocabulary words in context.

Grades 4 and 5 students will be able to:

+ Write a script and produce their own video.

+ Describe how air temperature, barometric pressure, wind speed, humidity, and precipitation determine the weather.

- Explain why different environments have varying climates.
- Distinguish between different types of precipitation.
- Use science content vocabulary in context.

Preparation

Materials:

- Weather Forecast Project Rubric (**bit.ly/3eSUMQX**)
- Video of meteorologists
- Video of meteorologists in severe weather
- Video creation tool (iMovie, Apple Clips, WeVideo, or similar)
- Props (rain ponchos, winter hats, umbrellas, and so on)
- Green screen

Standards Implemented in Lesson 1.1

ISTE STANDARDS FOR EDUCATORS	ISTE STANDARDS FOR STUDENTS	CONTENT STANDARDS
Citizen 3a, 3c Designer 5b Facilitator 6d	Digital Citizen 2c Knowledge Constructor 3a Innovative Designer 4c Creative Communicator 6b, 6c, 6d Global Collaborator 7c	Students will learn science weather and climate content. Severe weather safety, weather, and climate will be explored. To practice ELA writing skills, students will write descriptive narrative scripts designed for their intended audience.

Advanced Preparation:

✦ Gather examples of meteorologists providing the news during severe weather.

✦ Book your school's TV production studio or purchase a pop-up green screen (you can also use green or blue fabric).

✦ Teach students how to take notes or to sketchnote while reading articles and watching videos.

Instructions

Explain to students that they will have the opportunity to become junior meteorologists. Show video examples of meteorologists and severe weather. Ask students to work in groups to create a list of things they notice about meteorologists, along with a list of words that they use. Ask them to circle unknown vocabulary words. Display the Weather Forecast Project Rubric. Students will need to include a certain number of weather vocabulary words, along with a certain number of severe weather safety tips (the rubric is editable based on grade level and ability of your students). The rubric serves as an anticipation guide or variation on a K-W-L chart. It helps your students understand what they need to learn, and which word meanings they need to pay attention to or look up in a dictionary.

Provide weather content using your science textbook, BrainPOP videos, YouTube weather videos, and other relevant mini-lessons. Ask students to take notes while they watch the videos and read. During one or two class periods, provide students with time to conduct research on severe weather safety tips for their group's severe weather choice (blizzard, flood, hurricane, tornado, etc.). This a good opportunity to teach students effective research skills such as

Boolean logic, finding valid sources, and creating citations. It is also a good time to use the Check-in Journals you will read about later in Chapter 6. Students can use a digital tool, such as Flipgrid or Padlet, or write on paper and upload their journal entry later. The purpose is to encourage students to reflect on what they accomplished during the class period and what they still need to complete.

During one or two class periods, provide students with time to begin storyboarding and writing their scripts. This is typically when I begin working with one group at a time to choose the music for their news introduction. I use **incompetech.com** to find copyright-friendly songs. Students can also create their own music using a program such as GarageBand. When students finish writing their scripts and storyboards, ask them to create a list of props needed for their video. After you approve their script, students can begin recording their videos.

Next, students will edit their videos, adding news music, effects, and green-screen backgrounds.

Ask students to peer review each other's videos using Flipgrid, Padlet, or a similar tool. Students will use the project's rubric, as well as the Praise, Question, and Polish method to conduct their peer reviews (see Chapter 3 for more information about this strategy).

Students will edit videos based on their feedback.

Students will publish their weather forecast videos to be played on the morning announcements, shared on the school website, or shared with other classes globally.

Extensions

You could facilitate a videoconference with a meteorologist, allowing students to ask questions and gain more information to use in their videos.

ONLINE AND REMOTE LEARNING ADAPTATION

During a class videoconference, explain to students that they will become junior meteorologists, and show an example of a weather forecast. Students watch videos, read articles, and conduct additional research online to help them develop a script. Students can use Microsoft Word online or Google Docs to collaborate during script writing. Students plan sound effects for the weather they will be depicting and record a podcast of their weather forecast using a tool such as GarageBand, Vocaroo, or Padlet with audio. Students use their sound effects to simulate a radio weather forecast and publish their audio recording in an LMS, Padlet, Flipgrid, or other online platform.

LESSON PLAN 1.2 Hacking Science Labs

Subject: Science

Target Grades: K–12

Duration: 3 hours

Students will complete science labs and document them with YouTube-style videos. Students will use content vocabulary terms and work through the scientific process while explaining their hypothesis, materials, observations, and results.

Objectives

Grade K–5 students will be able to:

✦ Explain and use the scientific process.

✦ Use science content vocabulary in context.

✦ Complete a lab and explain the results.

✦ Compare their process and results with those from other groups.

Standards Implemented in Lesson 1.2

ISTE STANDARDS FOR EDUCATORS	ISTE STANDARDS FOR STUDENTS	CONTENT AREA STANDARDS
Citizen 3a, 3c Designer 5b Facilitator 6d	Digital Citizen 2c Creative Communicator 6b, 6c, 6d Global Collaborator 7c	Students will have the opportunity to practice using the scientific process while conducting labs and experiments. Students will explore grade-level science content through hands-on labs, while practicing speaking skills and using vocabulary in context.

Grade 6–12 students will be able to:

+ Explain and use the scientific process.

+ Conduct an investigation or experiment and evaluate the experimental design.

+ Use science content vocabulary in context.

+ Explain how a scientific investigation is replicable (or not).

+ Distinguish between replication and repetition (repeated trials).

Preparation

Materials:

+ Video creation tool (iMovie, Clips, WeVideo, or similar)

+ Scientific Process and Lab Guide (**bit.ly/2TAsGSL**)

+ Science Lab Rubric and Checklist (Elementary) (**bit.ly/3bVLvq5**)

+ Science Lab Investigation Rubric (Secondary) (**bit.ly/38haWC0**)

+ Various science materials for labs

+ Collaboration script: Science Lab Talking Prompts (**bit.ly/2XsqoYy**)

Advanced Preparation:

+ Prepare stations for the lab. (This works best during station rotations, unless you are able to provide headsets for students to block out background noise.)

+ Print or distribute digital copies of the Scientific Process and Lab Guide

Instructions

Before beginning the lab, review lab safety and the scientific process.

Describe the lab, and ask students to write their question ("What am I trying to figure out?"). Ask students to work with their partner or group to form a hypothesis and/or define a problem. Provide students with the collaboration script or talking prompts to help them communicate during the lab. The goal is that students will eventually be able to communicate without the script as they participate in more labs throughout the year.

If students haven't used it before, provide an overview of the video software they will use to create their lab demonstration video. Ideally, you should give students a chance to test the necessary software or digital tools in a low-risk academic environment prior to this lesson. For example, students could use the video tool to create an "all about me" video or to interview a classmate.

Students conduct additional research and engage in discussions to discuss their hypothesis for the upcoming lab. Remind students that being a scientist doesn't mean you are always correct. Figuring out that a strategy or experiment doesn't work is still a discovery and useful to other scientists.

Ask students to create digital posters or title slides for the sections of their video (Question, Hypothesis, Materials, Experiment, Results, Analysis). Secondary students should also demonstrate their ability to prepare a lab report.

Ask students to record themselves explaining their question and hypothesis.

Pass out lab materials, lab coats, and safety goggles.

Ask students to record themselves while conducting the experiment or investigation. Remind them to review their rubric and that they will need to use at least the required number of content vocabulary words while making observations about what they see. Ask students to record themselves explaining their results and analyzing the experiment (Figure 1.2). Students should state whether their hypothesis is correct.

1.2 Students at Wadsworth Elementary document their Force and Motion Lab using Apple's Clips app.

 During the next class period, provide time for students to finish editing their videos.

 Students post their videos in their LMS or other video hosting platform and make comparisons about the observations and results in the labs conducted by their peers. Students will create comments to address similarities and differences, as well as identify errors in reasoning.

For secondary classrooms, students will also evaluate the experimental design and describe how the lab could be repeated and/or replicated.

Address misconceptions and errors and relate the lab to previous content from the course. You can also show clips from various labs and pose questions to help students gain a deeper understanding of the content.

Extensions

Students use a tool such as Flipgrid to share their labs. Then they can partner with another class in the school or globally to share and compare videos, while discussing the importance of repeated trials to ensure that an an experiment's results are valid.

ONLINE AND REMOTE LEARNING ADAPTATION

Science labs will be tricky to incorporate in an online learning environment. However, if you think creatively you might be able to make this happen. Develop or find a lab that can be completed using household objects. I recommend surveying students and/or parents prior to the lesson to ensure that they have the materials needed to conduct the lab. One elementary example is to ask students to create a bubble wand to practice states of matter concepts. Discuss their background knowledge with blowing bubbles using a wand, and show a short video clip of the technique. Provide a recipe for the bubble solution, and ask students to locate household objects they can use to create a bubble wand. Students will use Flipgrid or Seesaw to record themselves engaging in the scientific process and testing their bubble wand. Students will reply to other videos and make comparisons about the different wands and how well they worked to produce bubbles. For older students, the American Association of Chemistry Teachers (AACT) published a list of take-home chemistry labs for high school students. You can find them at **bit.ly/2DJfXIs**.

LESSON PLAN 1.3 **Book Trailers**

Subject: ELA

Target Grades: K–12

Duration: 1–2 weeks

Students will create their own 60-second book trailers to provide details about a book they read, while encouraging other students to read the book. A great way to promote literacy, a book trailer consists of a short video that highlights the plot of a story or novel (without giving away the ending) and encourages others to read the book. You can use this project to review theme, plot, figurative language, and other literary elements.

Objectives

Grades K–5 students will be able to:

+ Provide details about a story or novel they read.

+ Clearly communicate a message.

+ Write, film, and edit videos.

+ Design backgrounds and graphics that support the theme and mood of their book.

Grade 6–12 students will be able to:

+ Write to convey a message and/or set a tone or mood.

+ Identify theme, plot, character development, point of view, and literary elements that help make the book engaging and/or effective in its message.

+ Write, film, and edit videos.

+ Design backgrounds and graphics that support the theme and mood of their book.

Standards Implemented in Lesson 1.3

ISTE STANDARDS FOR EDUCATORS	ISTE STANDARDS FOR STUDENTS	CONTENT STANDARDS
Citizen 3a, 3c Designer 5b Facilitator 6d	Digital Citizen 2c Knowledge Constructor 3a Innovative Designer 4c Creative Communicator 6b, 6c, 6d Global Collaborator 7c	Students will use ELA standards while writing their scripts, demonstrating detailed writing and grammatical skills. Students will also explore story sequencing, author's purpose, theme, and other literary elements.

Preparation

Materials:

✦ Video and editing software (iMovie, Clips, WeVideo, or similar)

✦ Movie Making Resources (**bit.ly/2ZsPLe2**)

✦ Paper and drawing or painting supplies

Instructions

 Show students examples of professional book trailers and other student-created book trailers. I usually show one example that is live action (students on camera acting) and one that shows slides or paper backgrounds with a student voice-over describing the pictures. Students could also choose to combine these two types of trailers. Ask students to share what they noticed about the book trailers. Create a list of their observations to display. Explain the characteristics of a book trailer (targets an audience, highlights a book, is short in length, doesn't give away the ending).

Divide students into groups of two to four, and provide time for each group to brainstorm ideas for books they can use. Tell students something like, "You may have a favorite book, but if it isn't easy to re-create on film or you can't think of any creative ways to talk about it, then it might be better to go with another option."

Provide mini-lessons to remind students about their writing skills, such as elaboration and providing details.

Students write their scripts and storyboards (for K–2 they could just create a storyboard) and submit it to you for approval. During this time, meet with one group at a time to help them select music that will play for the intro and background of their trailer. After receiving approval for their scripts and storyboards, students create a prop list.

Students record their book trailers and create their title slides and background images. Students edit their book trailers, adding relevant special effects, title slides, music, and voice-overs (if applicable).

 Students post their video trailers in their LMS, Seesaw, Flipgrid, or another video hosting platform. Students peer review other book trailers and provide feedback.

Students make revisions based on feedback.

 Students publish their book trailers on school announcements, at the book fair, on the class website, or on another online platform.

Extensions

To take publishing to another level, you can create a student film festival complete with a red carpet, popcorn, and paparazzi (teachers dressed in all black with cameras). I recommend selecting ten to twelve videos from different genres to be shown in their entirety. You can also create a montage of the other videos to show in one clip, so all student-created videos are represented during the event. Students can be encouraged to dress up in order to make the event feel more special. When I have helped initiate events like this, they are always a big hit with parents, teachers, and especially students. For secondary students, make them part of the process and empower them to create the film festival and select the films that will be shown during the event.

ONLINE AND REMOTE LEARNING ADAPTATION

During a class videoconference, show examples of a book trailer and explain the project. Students choose books for their book trailers and then begin writing their scripts. Students use their devices to create a book trailer. (Note: As students may not have a family member to help, they can create drawings to depict the book and then record their voice for the book trailer, rather than creating a live action film.) Students select music and effects for their book trailer and submit it to the class LMS or other video hosting platform. Students conduct peer reviews and engage in the revision process. Students display their published book trailers on the school website or on a Google Site.

COACH'S CONNECTION

As district or school-level educational technology coaches, we have the opportunity to provide instruction in areas beyond technology. Coaches are often well connected and have access to resources and ideas that teachers have not experienced. Although technology integration is the primary focus of our role, I recommend prioritizing other areas that can be included in model lessons, professional learning, and coaching sessions.

Each Coach's Connection in this book incorporates ways coaches can support teachers in implementing the concepts and project ideas described in each chapter. Although the content was designed for edtech coaches, there is valuable information that any educator can use. Chapter 1 discusses ways to include culturally responsive teaching in lessons and projects, as well as creating a classroom culture that is conducive to projects. This Coach's Connection provides ideas to help teachers evaluate the level of cultural responsiveness in their classroom and explores ways coaches can model and assist teachers in building a positive classroom culture.

Encourage Culturally Responsive Teaching

Many teachers feel they are proficient at representing and responding to cultural diversity in their classrooms, when in fact they have much room for growth. Your challenge as a coach is to help teachers identify their needs in this area, without upsetting them or making them feel inadequate.

One strategy is to enlist the teacher's help in meeting your own goals. Show them the Change Agent and Collaborator standards (ISTE Standards for Coaches, 1b, 3b, 2019):

+ Change Agent 1b: Facilitate equitable use of digital learning tools and content that meets the needs of each learner.

+ Collaborator 3b: Partner with educators to identify digital learning content that is culturally relevant, developmentally appropriate and aligned to content standards.

Inform the teachers that these are goals you are working toward this year, and ask if they are willing to volunteer to help evaluate their own progress in these areas, identifying any areas that could be improved. When teachers understand that your sessions are truly a collaboration, they will be more willing to participate. If you start with a handful of willing teachers in each school, the ideas will naturally spread as teachers collaborate with their peers.

Here are two ideas for getting started with evaluating your current digital tools and content for cultural responsiveness:

+ Work collaboratively with teachers to evaluate the most common technology apps or websites they use with their students. When working together to develop a technology-infused project, use the Culturally Responsive Curriculum Scorecard (**bit.ly/CRTscorecard**) to determine if the lesson is welcoming to all students and meets their individual needs. Even if you are only able to complete this process once or twice per year with the selected teachers, this should help them begin thinking about how inclusive they are in their own lessons and curriculum choices, and will prompt more global changes in their classrooms (NYU Metro Center, 2020).

+ Survey students to determine their level of comfort and belonging in their classroom. Even students as young as kindergarten and first grade should be able to indicate if they feel safe and happy to visit their classroom each day. If students indicate discomfort, a further level of investigation will be needed and perhaps classroom changes.

Perhaps the most significant impact you can make is to model culturally responsive practices for the teachers you coach. For example, when scheduling guest speakers and videoconferences, consider how you can help students learn from culturally diverse adults. If, despite your district's best efforts, a school's student and teacher population do not align in terms of race and culture, bringing in diverse guest speakers is an important step to connect students with adults who look like them. Likewise, in your professional development training, consider how you can promote an inclusive environment for all participants. Following groups and conversations that regularly incorporate culturally responsive teaching, diversity, and community is another good source of ideas. Here are a few good resources;

if you know of others, please share them using the book's hashtag, #AuthenticEdVentures:

- ✦ ISTE Connect Digital Equity Network. For ISTE members, this community offers challenging conversations and resources to help address equity issues and culturally responsive teaching. To access this network, log in to ISTE and visit **bit.ly/2ZXPMqd**. Scroll down, place a check next to the Digital Equity Network, and then save.

- ✦ #FLedChat. Hosted by Dene Gainey, this Twitter chat features discussions about diversity and community at 8 p.m. (ET) on the fourth Wednesday of each month. You can locate this chat on Twitter using the hashtag #FLedChat.

- ✦ All Y'all Social Justice Collective. Comprised of educators from the southeastern U.S., this organization offers an annual series of professional learning experiences focused on culturally responsive teaching and other social justice topics. Visit **allyalledu.com** to learn more.

Some of these suggestions probably seem like common sense or ideas that are already in place in your school or district. Unless we are intentionally planning to incorporate culturally responsive teaching, however, it probably is not happening across all classrooms or as often as we think. It is understandable if you do not feel like an expert in this. Neither do I—and that's good! Often when we feel like we "should" already be an expert at something, lifelong learning halts. Instead, model the behavior you want your teachers to model for their students: Embrace the opportunity to learn from others, be vulnerable, and share your vulnerability with your teachers too. We are all still learning in this project together.

Following up is just as important as starting conversations. Meet with your teachers once or twice a year to evaluate current practices in this area and discuss future plans. A few simple changes or additions will go a long way toward preparing an environment where students feel comfortable working together.

Model a Positive Culture in Your Coaching

To be successful, the most important thing a coach needs to do is build trust in their teachers. The ISTE Standards for Coaches are quite clear on that. As indicator 1a of the Change Agent standard states, coaches should "cultivate a supportive coaching culture that encourages educators and leaders to achieve a shared vision and individual goals" (ISTE, 2019). Additionally, indicator 3a of the Collaborator standard states that coaches should build "trusting and respectful coaching relationships that encourage educators to explore new instructional strategies" (ISTE, 2019).

Having been a teacher myself, I know the difference between coaches you could confide in and those who simply point out all the areas where you need to improve. Modeling a constructive, collaborative culture can inspire teachers to establish similar connections with their students, ultimately creating an environment more conducive to project-based learning. To help build strong bonds with your teachers, always keep these principles in mind:

+ A coach is not an evaluator. For teachers to truly learn and grow from our sessions, coaching should not feel like a "gotcha." Teachers need to feel that you are there to work together, rather than to judge their teaching or to run tattling to school administrators. Even when you are tasked with conducting a formal evaluation, I recommend asking administrators that the results be shared between you and the teacher rather than included in an official school evaluation.

+ During coaching sessions in which I observe and provide feedback, I try to ask questions and help teachers determine their own areas of need. Most of the time they understand the areas they need to improve in, just not how to make it happen. This is where you can come in, trying different strategies to help solve common classroom challenges. Phrases like, "I have this idea that might work. Maybe we can pilot this strategy with your students? What do you think," let teachers know that you do not have all the answers either. You're two educators brainstorming together to try something new, which makes finding a working solution more likely. Many of the ideas included in this book started out this way.

+ Coaching sessions should be kept confidential (within reason). Teachers talk . . . a lot! Teachers will confide in you, and sometimes you will observe lessons that are epic fails or days where the teacher is unprepared. Remember, you are not their supervisor or evaluator. You are there to support and provide guidance. If you break the trust of a teacher by talking about things that should be kept confidential, it is highly probable that this news will spread across the school rapidly, and gaining teacher trust will be more difficult in the future. If you witness something truly concerning relating to student safety and/or well-being, however, then it is your obligation to report it.

+ Coaching is a service position. Our challenge as coaches is to inspire and share information. With that information in hand, it is the teacher's decision on how to proceed from there. As coaches we get to be a salesperson of sorts, providing our pitch and then sitting back to watch how teachers run with the ideas we share. For example, I do gently push at times, helping to convince teachers that their students are capable of more or that technology can be used more, for purposes other than drill and practice. When you approach coaching as a position of authority and dictate to teachers what they need to do, however, you will not be as effective and will certainly not build lasting relationships.

+ Coaching is collaborative. When you approach coaching as a collaborative process, the personalization naturally falls into place. The Connected Learner standard states that coaches should "establish shared goals with educators, reflect on successes and continually improve coaching and teaching practice" (ISTE Standards for Coaches, 2c, 2019). The Collaborator standard elaborates, stating that coaches should "personalize support for educators by planning and modeling the effective use of technology to improve student learning" (ISTE Standards for Coaches, 3d, 2019).

✦ Setting shared goals can seem like a daunting task; however, a couple resources that can help you find technology tools and activities that align to create effective strategies for the classroom are the ISTE Course of Mind Initiative (**bit.ly/2AdI2G5**) and COSN Hurdles and Accelerators Report (**bit.ly/2AlQfI9**). Created in collaboration with ISTE and Chan Zuckerberg, the Course of Mind Initiative seeks to provide educators with the latest brain-based research, combining the knowledge and talents from neuroscientists, psychologists, computer scientists, educators, and other experts to provide learning science insights. Formerly called the Horizon Report, the COSN Hurdles and Accelerators Report details current trends and hurdles we are facing in K–12 educational technology.

As coaches, our job is to support teachers and help them be successful—whether they need to laugh, cry, vent, or just feel like they are not in it alone. Walk beside them, not above them, and remember how challenging their role can be amongst constant changes, increased pressure and expectations, and constant reminders (especially via social media) of how others are doing more.

 As we move into Chapter 2, I encourage you to share how your project mindset has evolved. How do you plan to incorporate student goal setting and culturally responsive practices in your own classroom or with the coaches you serve? Let me and your fellow readers know using the hashtag #AuthenticEdVentures.

CREATING CREATIVE COMMUNICATORS

In nearly any career path our students choose, they will need to deliver presentations or speeches, whether describing their skills in a job interview, marketing their employer's brand on social media, or collaborating with colleagues around the world via videoconference tools. Combining opportunities for practice with lessons about design principles will better prepare students for whatever their futures hold.

Gone are the days when a high-quality presentation meant a deck of template-based Microsoft PowerPoint slides with bullet points and flashy animations. Social media and YouTube are bursting with great examples including TED Talks, PechaKucha presentations (more on this later), reviews, demonstrations, and speeches. With such a variety of examples available (of what to avoid as well as to emulate), it's easier than ever to teach students about the multimedia and the design principles they need to create effective slideshows, videos, or live presentations for their projects.

Understanding design principles will also help you and your students evaluate their presentations to determine the extent to which they are increasing cognitive load and potentially reducing learning retention. *Cognitive load* is the amount of information our working memory can hold while attempting to learn a skill or concept. If cognitive load is too large—full of distractions from the main point, unfamiliar content vocabulary, an abundance of new information, and so on—just like an overfilled grocery bag, items start spilling out rather than reaching the destination of our long-term memory storage cupboard. Whether you're designing lessons for your students or they are designing presentations for their peers, your goals are the same: to reduce cognitive load and ensure that the important information makes it from the audience's working memory into their long-term memory.

Helping students learn presentation design principles and better understand what causes excessive cognitive load will help them evaluate the content they regularly read or view and increase their learning outcomes in any area. By teaching these skills you are actually empowering your students to take charge of their learning and to make changes when effective learning conditions are not in place. In this chapter, we will explore ways to teach these skills and more principles of effective presentation design and delivery, as well as discuss how to engage and motivate students to do their best work—even those who are uncomfortable presenting to an audience.

Motivate Students to Create Quality Work

Great speakers and presenters aren't simply knowledgeable about their topics, they are also highly motivated and willing to put in hours of practice. They care about the quality of their work. Although many students care as well, an equal number do just enough to fulfill a rubric or achieve a required grade. Observing smart and studious, yet disengaged, students over the years has made me realize that too often we are teaching students to check boxes and follow routines, rather than helping them to become lifelong learners. No wonder many teachers struggle with getting quality work from their students. When it comes to presentations, that struggle can be intensified by student anxieties surrounding speaking in front of an audience.

Aside from time, getting students to complete quality work can be one of the biggest challenges teachers face. Sometimes, however, just a few small tweaks to assignments and projects can help encourage quality work from students, even reticent ones. For example, here are some effective ways to encourage students to take pride in their work:

✦ Allow student choice. Whenever possible, provide opportunities for your students to choose what they learn, how they learn, and how they demonstrate their learning. Opportunities can range from their choice of project topics to where and how they conduct their research to how they present their projects. This process takes time, however, as many students are used to being told what to do by teachers. You can start by providing options, and later move toward more open-ended choices. Involve students in the project-design process by surveying them. Ask, "How do you best learn?", "What would make you more engaged in this class?", "How do you learn things outside of class?", and similar questions. I have been amazed at how much insight students are able to provide and how much they understand about good teaching and the ways they most effectively learn. Even if you are unable to use many of their ideas, students will appreciate you gathering feedback and listening.

+ Use models. Project examples and models help students visualize what they are expected to create. You could even create a mediocre example project and then ask students to score it using the project rubric. Ask them how they would improve the quality of the project and how the project could earn a higher score on the rubric. Much like peer review, this evaluation process helps students begin to think about their own project and how they can ensure that they are turning in high-quality work. To help me remember past projects and provide authentic examples to share with students year after year, I take photos of student work and save them in a Google Drive folder titled Student Work that is divided into subfolders for various categories of work.

+ Provide clear expectations. Clearly defined expectations help students produce quality work. In addition, you need to provide expectations that are challenging but achievable, and possibly even differentiated from student to student or group to group. To help you home in on these "just right" expectations, think of your favorite game. A good game is challenging, but not so much that you feel defeated by its complexity, nor is it too easy so you quickly become bored. Good video games also provide scaffolding in the forms of hints and animated "helpers." If you don't strike the sweet spot of expectations the first time, you're not alone. Creating "game-like" expectations with the optimal levels of challenge and support can be an iterative process. It will probably take some adjustments, and you may find you need to inform students that you are adding an extra challenge or scaling back your original rubric. It is better to make adjustments than to continue with a project that frustrates your students or is too simplistic. Another good practice is to display expectations in writing and refer back to them frequently. With younger students, I provide a checklist instead of a rubric, or in addition to it. This helps ensure that they are meeting expectations.

+ Another good practice is to ask students to explain the expectations via Flipgrid or a similar video discussion platform, enabling other students to fill in the gaps when their peers are not clear about the project expectations. When students can learn from each other, rather than always hearing everything from their teachers, they take valuable steps toward independence and self-regulation.

+ Provide an authentic audience. Students value feedback, and it is even more important if the feedback is relevant and from an authentic source. For example, when implementing a project to help protect bees, students can interview a local beekeeper to gather information. If students are designing a tiny house, an architect can review their plans and offer ideas. Chapter 3 includes more information about how to incorporate an authentic audience into your projects.

+ Make time for revision. The process of revision can be tedious but also rewarding. As teachers, we often forget to include time for this process in our project plans. Revision can also feel overwhelming to some students who are unsure where or how to start. Provide guidance for this in the form of rubrics, checklists, and even modeling. Depending on the project, you may even want to include multiple revisions for various components. For example, when creating a book trailer (Lesson Plan 1.3), students will need to review their script, adding details and clarifying any confusing parts. They will also need to review their footage and editing, maybe adding additional special effects, reshooting any parts with shaky camera work, and so on. For other projects, one revision might be sufficient. The revision phase would also be a good time to bring a live or virtual guest author or artist to discuss their own revision process.

ENGAGE SHY AND INTROVERTED STUDENTS

Many students become excited at the idea of talking in class, collaborating with other students, and taking center stage while they deliver their presentations. Others, however, cringe or experience anxiety just thinking about face-to-face presentations. One way to lessen this anxiety is to engage students in short presentations that take place in front of small groups of students, rather than an entire class. A great opportunity for this type of practice is Speed Dating presentations, in which a student presents one-on-one to a rotating set of partners (see the "Engage Students in Intentional Practice" section for more details). Another is Jigsaw cooperative learning, in which groups of students are each responsible for researching a specific portion of a larger topic and then teaching the other groups about it. For example, while teaching a unit on the human body, you assign the respiratory system to one group, the circulatory system to another, and so on. Each group then conducts research and creates a strategy to teach their content to the other groups. Later, students rotate through each group, presenting their content. (Lesson Plan 2.2 is another example of a Jigsaw project.) Because they are less formal and allow students to get comfortable presenting in front of a small group before attempting to present to a larger audience, both Speed Dating and Jigsaw projects are excellent ways to ease shy or nervous students into presenting content in front of their peers.

Giving students the option to deliver their presentations online is another way to meet the needs of shy or introverted students. I have often witnessed students who are extremely shy during face-to-face activities blossom when they are able to create audio or video recordings or other online content. This is where some students shine and are able to formulate their thoughts and deliver their ideas in a comfortable setting. These same students may also excel in presentations in which they play a character and act, rather than presenting as themselves. (Just remember that others, like me, may become anxious or awkward under the impersonal stare of a camera lens or microphone.)

I saw a prime example of the positive effects of online presentations about five years ago: After instructing a group of third graders about participating in discussions via their learning management system, I returned for a follow-up visit a few days later. The teacher excitedly pulled me aside to share that a student who never talked in class was creating poised and eloquent video tutorials in response to his classmates' questions about how to use the LMS. His teacher and I were thrilled and surprised at how well-spoken he was. Had we not provided this alternate venue (although accidentally) for the student to express himself, we would never have known. Subsequently, he opened up more in class, as students thanked him for his videos and expressed how good he was at presenting in his tutorials. Online collaboration platforms not only provide opportunities for students to express themselves but also for the extroverted students to appreciate ideas contributed by their less talkative classmates. Some specific ideas for engaging students in online presentations will be discussed in Chapter 6.

HELP STUDENTS UNDERSTAND THE IMPORTANCE OF DESIGN

To create and deliver effective presentations, students need to understand more than how to be motivated, comfortable speakers or how to produce slideshows and recordings. They need to understand the importance of good design, how to craft their own designs effectively, and that practice is a vital component to a successful presentation. Sharing the following activities and design tips with students *before* they develop their presentation slides, videos, and infographics will help them produce their best-quality work.

Design is all around us, and we have no choice but to pay attention to it on a daily basis—whether we're conscious of it or not. When presented with marketing for any product, for example, we each gravitate toward certain colors, fonts, music, and styles. Often the way a product's packaging looks, the way it presents itself, determines whether we want to buy it or not.

When engaging in project-based learning, students will benefit from learning that marketing can be as important as the product. Whether students are trying to persuade an audience about a cause or to sell a product, they will learn the important role design plays in this process. One or both of the activities in this section can serve as an introduction to student presentations, helping them see the importance of design and the impact it has on marketing and other areas of life.

+ Snack Challenge. Select a cookie or other snack that is available in one or more well-known brands with flashy, well-designed packaging and several other generic brands with more plainly designed packaging. Chocolate chip cookies, potato chips, or cola would work. At first, show students the various packages only. Ask them to predict which product will taste better and to write a short reflection about why they think they will like that one the best. Next, provide students with a sample of each brand in plain, individual containers labeled 1, 2, and 3. Ask them to taste each and select their favorite. If they like or dislike them all equally, ask them to indicate that as well. After all students have indicated their selections and reasoning, show them which brand was in which numbered container. Discuss how the packaging and branding design affected their initial choice. Talk about other packaging designs that influence their buying decisions. Students will become more conscious about the role that marketing has in our world.

+ Analyze a Keynote. Select a TED Talk that you feel will be interesting to all (or at least most of) your students. As they watch the keynote, ask them to consider:

  + What makes this person a "great" speaker?

  + What makes this speech interesting and enjoyable?

  + What specific practices does this person use to keep the audience interested and entertained?

  + What features make their presentation slides interesting and easy to understand?

+ Play about 3–5 minutes of the speech, then pause and review the questions. Ask students to begin writing what they noticed so far, and then play more of the video. Depending on the attention span and ability level of your students, you may need to pause three to eight times. Next, discuss your students' findings and realizations. Create a chart listing the observations your students made. Use these observations to create a list of guidelines for your students' projects. Involving students in this process helps them feel ownership of the goals they are working toward. This activity will most likely take one class period, but the potential benefits will help them throughout the school year and beyond.

Design Tips Based on Mayer's Principles of Multimedia Learning

Richard Mayer is an educational psychologist who, among many other contributions to theories of cognition and learning, developed a series of best practices for designing content to meet the needs of learners (Mayer, 2008). Not only can these easily be adapted into helpful design tips for students creating and delivering presentations, but also, using these principles in your own lesson content will serve as a great model for students. We as teachers become frustrated during professional learning sessions that promote collaborative learning, differentiated instruction, and other effective strategies all while the presenter reads the same slideshow bullet points to an entire school staff during a lecture. Students feel the same way when we deliver instruction using poorly designed slides that lack proper citations. If this is an area of weakness for you, I encourage you to be transparent about this to your students and let them know that you are learning together and all striving to become better creative communicators using the same principles:

+ You're giving a presentation, not a document. Reading bullet points on slides, particularly when stumbling on words, makes it clear to the audience that you are not knowledgeable about the topic or do not feel confident talking freely. If there are certain aspects of your presentation that you feel your audience will need to reference later, then create a separate document to give them at the end of your session. This document can include strategies, links, tips, and so on. Now your presentation can consist of well-designed slides with interesting and relevant visual aids. When providing students with expectations for their presentations, make it clear that reading bullet points is not acceptable. You can share examples of various presentations, and ask students to sort them into categories such as heartwarming, inspiring, or informative. Later, students can explain why they liked some and not others. This is an excellent introduction to begin your conversation about the importance of multimedia and design principles.

+ Use text effectively—and not too often. Mayer's Modality Principle explains that when you display a graphic, people process its information better through hearing it described aloud, rather than reading on-screen text (2008). Think of it this way: Would you rather watch a movie with easy-to-understand dialogue or one that requires the distraction or cognitive challenge of reading subtitles while trying to follow the on-screen action? If you decide to incorporate on-screen text into your presentation, consider using the Signaling Principle, which promotes the benefits of highlighting the organization of key terms and ideas (Mayer, 2008), literally signaling to the learner, "Hey, this is important." BrainPOP videos are a great example of reducing on-screen text and using both sound and bold text, while highlighting to signal key information to students.

+ Exclude irrelevant content. Graphic designers often promote the importance of white space, while fashion icon Coco Chanel famously instructed, "Before you leave the house, look in the mirror and take one thing off." Both these "less is more" sentiments are in accordance with Mayer's Coherence Principle, which explains that extraneous sounds, pictures, and words can increase cognitive load (2008). Providing clear guidelines about "decorations" will help students—especially elementary students who are famous for adding glitter and gifs in any available space—begin to develop better design skills, which will benefit them in the future. So save the glitter for free art time, or better yet, save your custodial staff's sanity and skip it altogether.

+ Break it up. The Segmenting Principle states that students learn better when content is broken up into segments, rather than a continuous unit (Mayer, 2008). Just like good teachers provide time for practice, interaction, and other activities during a lecture, we can ask students to do this in their presentations as well.

PRACTICE MAYER'S MULTIMEDIA PRINCIPLES WITH PECHAKUCHA

PechaKucha is an ideal presentation style for teaching students about the importance of delivery. Often called 20 X 20 presentations, PechaKucha presentations are 6 minutes long, containing 20 slides that are presented for 20 seconds each. Slides automatically advance, which encourages presenters to practice and ensures that they can summarize slide content in the allotted time. The lack of text also encourages practice and being thoroughly confident with your content. PechaKucha emphasizes storytelling, rather than reading prepared bullet points. Although a 20-slide presentation is appropriate for secondary students who have been given adequate time to prepare, you may decide to reduce this to 10, 5, or even 3 slides for an elementary class. You could also use a version with 1 to 3 slides for short-research projects in any grade level, providing students with 15 to 20 minutes in class to conduct research and present about a concept or vocabulary word at the end of class. As an alternative, students could use this method to summarize content from a mini-lesson that you taught earlier in a class period.

The official PechaKucha website (**pechakucha.com**) provides more information and many example presentations, as well as a freemium template that allows presenters to practice with the auto-advanced slides. However, you can easily create a template in Microsoft PowerPoint, Keynote, or Google Slides, or you can use the 20-slide template I provide with Lesson 2.1. (Google Slides templates are a little tricky to create because you can't create slide timings without first publishing the slideshow to the web.) I recommend checking out the PechaKucha website to find events near you, as well as online examples to share with your students. One of my favorite examples is "The Morden [sic] Heirloom: Coding Quilts" by Elizabeth Elliott.

+ Use your voice. The Personalization Principle promotes the use of conversational, rather than formal, language during presentations. Research shows this promotes better learning outcomes (Mayer, 2008). So focus more on clarity, content, and confidence while your students are speaking, and let them use their voice. This applies to online presentations and podcasts as well. Using conversational language such as "I" and "you," as opposed to more formal vocabulary, keeps learners more interested.

Engage Students in Intentional Practice

To boost their clarity and confidence when presenting, students need to practice their delivery. When interviewed about their preparation process, many keynote speakers stated that they practice 10 times for a 25–30 minute presentation. For example, one speaker stated that she practiced her TED Talk 200 times, while others said they practice until the speech is effortless (Gallo, 2018). While it may be difficult to provide students with several class periods to prepare for a presentation of 5 or 10 minutes, it is important to provide at least some class time for practice. Here are a couple activities to help students practice their presentations during class time. As a bonus, they double as great opportunities to incorporate peer review into the project process. (Chapter 3 will discuss implementing peer reviews in more depth.)

+ Presentation Speed Dating. The Speed Dating technique is adaptable to any content. For presentations, have students select a 2-minute portion of their presentation to rehearse, such as a section they typically struggle with or one they feel could benefit from peer feedback. Ask for volunteers to travel from station to station as *guests*. A *host* student waits at each station. Each round of visits begins with the guest practicing their presentation segment. After the station's host provides feedback, the partners switch roles with the host practicing and the guest giving feedback. Each round should last about 6 minutes and allow about 30 seconds of transition time for the guests to move to another station. Students can either offer open feedback (my preference), which provides students with more insight into the specific areas they need to improve upon, or feedback based on a rubric's checklist. Students will check areas that need improvement and areas of strengths in each presentation. You could also provide reflection time for the presenter before switching roles, allowing them to consider the feedback they received and make immediate changes. Speed Dating presentations can be adapted for an online learning environment by asking the host students to create videoconference sessions that the guests can rotate through during presentation rounds.

✦ Flipgrid Feedback. If face-to-face feedback is not an option, consider using a tool such as Flipgrid to provide students with opportunities to practice. Have students record a practice session in Flipgrid, re-recording until they are satisfied with their video, and then post the video to a Flipgrid topic. Other students can later log in to Flipgrid, visit the topic, and provide video feedback for at least three other students. The Flipgrid Coach feature also provides students with feedback about their presentation and allows them to make edits. For example, it alerts them if they are speaking too fast or slowly, or saying "umm." The advantage of Flipgrid is that students can post their videos from home or school, any time of day.

If it is not practical to provide at least one class period for presentation preparation, then consider foregoing homework for a period of time, allowing students time to practice at home. Be sure to model good practicing techniques and provide students with clear expectations. For example, Gallo (2018) notes that many professional speakers practice in front of an audience and even record their presentations to catch errors they were not aware of.

CITATIONS AND FAIR USE GUIDELINES

Some students learn the hard way, like the sixth-graders I met last year who posted YouTube videos featuring copyrighted music on their paid channel, only to later receive a message that their video was removed due to copyright violations. After they continued to post similar videos, the site suspended their channel. Providing students with copyright and citation instruction *prior* to their posting public content online or presenting in class is equally beneficial—and less painful.

For example, I begin by asking students to raise their hands if they have borrowed something from someone in the last week. Usually, only one or two students do. Next, I ask, "How many of you have watched a YouTube or other online video in the last week?" Typically, all or nearly all students raise their hands, and then we discuss that watching a YouTube video is essentially borrowing something from the creator. You will not need to "return" it, but it is still using something that does not belong to you. This easily leads into a conversation about providing credit for photos, music, and other files students use or remix in their schoolwork or daily lives.

It's never too early to start good habits: For example, I ask first-grade students to write the name of the website or book where they found the information for their posters or slides. This is fairly simple for them and helps them start thinking about the importance of providing credit. Another option would be to provide them with icons depicting the sources that you will be using, so they can copy and paste these on their slides or posters. If they are creating paper reports, you can print stickers for commonly used sources, such as DKfindout! and National Geographic Kids. Students will have fun putting the stickers on their paper and gain a rudimentary understanding of copyright expectations. I love the idea of mixing digital research with hands-on or paper presentations, especially in the primary grades.

LESSON PLANS

The following lessons provide opportunities for students to practice presentation skills and instructional design. You will notice that copyright guidelines are incorporated into project rubrics, and feedback in the form of peer review is also included.

LESSON PLAN 2.1 PechaKucha Presentations

Subject: Any content area

Target Grades: 2–12

Duration: 2–3 class periods

This lesson plan engages students in PechaKucha presentations to demonstrate their knowledge of concepts, while practicing speaking skills. You can select any content you would like students to present. PechaKucha presentations are typically presented individually, so this is one of the few lesson plans that doesn't incorporate cooperative learning until students engage in peer review.

Objectives

Grades 2–12 students will be able to:

+ Clearly and knowledgeably speak about their topic.
+ Create a well-designed presentation.
+ Answer questions related to their presentation topic.

Standards Implemented in Lesson 2.1

ISTE STANDARDS FOR EDUCATORS	ISTE STANDARDS FOR STUDENTS	CONTENT AREA STANDARDS
Citizen 3a, 3c Designer 5b Facilitator 6d	Digital Citizen 2c Knowledge Constructor 3a Innovative Designer 4c Creative Communicator 6b, 6c, 6d	Students will use ELA research and speaking and listening standards to gather information about a topic and present it to their peers. (Additional content standards can also be incorporated.)

Preparation

Materials:

✦ Google Slides Presentation Template (**bit.ly/36yQA6E**) or other presentation software template

✦ Nonfiction books and internet sources for student research

Advanced Preparation:

✦ Prepare a slideshow template with slides that automatically transition after 20 seconds. Note: The Google Slides Template includes 20 slides. If you plan to use fewer, you can delete the other slides. I recommend making a copy first, in case you would like to use more slides for a future presentation.

Instructions

 Explain the meaning of PechaKucha to students. Provide an example to show that is relevant to your students' interests. I recommend visiting the **pechakucha.com** website to find an example.

 Provide students time to begin researching their topic, which should be relevant to your course content. For example, if you were studying DNA and RNA, students would explore a topic related to those science concepts.

 Check student topics and research sources and approve them or ask questions to help students determine a better topic or more current and relevant sources. Provide time for students to conduct additional research and create their presentation slides.

  Provide students with time to practice their presentations.

  Provide students with time to engage in the peer review process. Students can perform their presentations live for other students or can record their presentations to post online for their reviewers to watch. Another option for shorter presentations (1–3 minutes) is the Speed Dating method, in which students move from classmate to classmate practicing their presentations.

  Provide students time to present their PechaKucha presentations either live or publish them online in a learning management system such as Canvas or Schoology.

Extensions

Host a live (coffeehouse-style) event for interested students to present their PechaKucha presentations. You may even find a coffeehouse or restaurant willing to host.

LESSON PLAN 2.2 Life Cycles Jigsaw Research Project

Subject: Science/ELA (could be adapted for other content areas)

Target Grades: K–5

Duration: 1 week

This lesson features one example of Jigsaw cooperative learning presentations. Although this particular lesson features an elementary-level life cycles topic, you could adapt it for nearly any grade level and content area. In fact, I have used a similar lesson with my college students. With this version of Jigsaw learning, students work in teams to teach others about their life cycle (e.g., a mammal, bird, or reptile). Students will work with their team members to research facts about their life cycle and draw a model of the life cycle to share with others.

Objectives

Grade K–2 students will be able to:

+ Explain, draw, and label one animal life cycle.

+ Effectively conduct research.

+ Compare two or more life cycles.

+ Work cooperatively to create a presentation that helps teach others about a topic.

Grade 3–5 students will be able to:

+ Explain the interdependence between their plant or animal and other living things.

+ Conduct effective research.

+ Compare two or more animal or plant life cycles and classify them.

+ Work cooperatively to create a presentation that helps teach others about a topic.

Standards Implemented in Lesson 2.2

ISTE STANDARDS FOR EDUCATORS	ISTE STANDARDS FOR STUDENTS	CONTENT AREA STANDARDS
Citizen 3b, 3c Designer 5b Facilitator 6a, 6d Analyst 7a	Digital Citizen 2c Knowledge Constructor 3a Innovative Designer 4c Creative Communicator 6b, 6c, 6d Global Collaborator 7c	Students will engage in ELA research standards, as well as science life cycles and animal habitat topics.

Preparation

Materials:

✦ Books and internet sources to research life cycles

✦ Digital or paper copies of the Life Cycle Template (**bit.ly/2ZtrzGU**)

✦ Colored pencils or crayons

Advanced Preparation:

✦ Copy life cycle templates or provide them in the student learning management system.

✦ Optional: Select a variety of animals that can easily be researched by students.

Instructions

 Explain to students that they will have the opportunity to be teachers and that their classmates will be relying on them for important information. Display the Life Cycles Template, and ask students to help you create a model example. As a class, research one life cycle and complete the diagram and fact sheet.

 Divide students into groups. Pair your students by ability (according to this particular topic and subject), trying to group students with similar abilities and academic knowledge). Provide students with their templates and rubric and ask them to help crowdsource a list of research tips and guidelines.

 Provide students with 45–60 minutes to create their lesson. They will need to make two copies of everything in their presentation, as some members of the team will stay at their desks (home team), and others will travel from group to group (traveling team).

 Students will continue conducting research, as well as collaborate on the fact sheet and life cycle drawing using tools such as Google Drawings.

 Provide students with time to practice their presentations and select the home and traveling team members. Ideally, you would have two home team members and two travelers, but there are variations for this. Review the Jigsaw procedures with students, i.e., how the home team will stay at their desks as the travelers move each round. I use an interval timer (see Chapter 6 for more details) to help manage the time for each round. Additionally, I remind students that the guests share first, and then the home team. Each round should last 5–8 minutes, depending on the age of your students and the length of their presentations. Between each round, provide groups 1–2 minutes to take notes. They will be using these later.

After all the rounds are complete, ask students to return to their original groups. This is the most important part of the lesson. Using their notes, students will complete a Venn diagram or similar graphic organizer to compare and contrast their life cycle with one or two others (depending on time).

Extensions

One extension is to allow high achievers or interested students the opportunity to create a multimedia file to share with the other groups. This can be a short video clip, song they create, photo collage, and/or any other ideas they have.

ONLINE AND REMOTE LEARNING ADAPTATION

Explain the life cycles project and assign topics during a synchronous videoconference session. Next, students will collaborate using Google Docs or Microsoft Word online, and, if possible, use videoconference breakout rooms or an online discussion to share ideas. They will conduct research and complete their fact sheets to align with the project checklist. Students will present their Jigsaw presentations using Flipgrid, Seesaw, their LMS, or another video hosting platform.

LESSON PLAN 2.3 **Math Jigsaw Project**

Subject: Math

Target Grades: 6–8

Duration: 2–3 days

This lesson features an example of Jigsaw cooperative learning presentations in your classroom. Although this particular lesson features middle-school math content, it could be adapted for nearly any grade level and content area. With this version of Jigsaw learning, students work in teams to teach others math concepts. For example, in a geometry lesson you could assign each group a topic, such as Measuring Angles in Degrees; Acute, Right, and Obtuse Angles; Vertical Angles; and Complementary and Supplementary Angles. Students rotate from group to group, learning the math concepts from their peers while you monitor the room, noting any misconceptions or errors in reasoning to be addressed later.

Objectives

Grades 6–8 students will be able to:

✦ Explain a math concept using visual and/or digital aids.

✦ Use math vocabulary in context.

✦ Construct viable arguments and critique the reasoning of others.

Preparation

Materials:

✦ Math textbook or other resources, such as Khan Academy or YouTube

✦ Math Jigsaw Rubric (**bit.ly/38r2osC**)

Advanced Preparation:

✦ Copy Math Jigsaw Rubric, or provide it in the student learning management system.

✦ Select topics for each group.

Standards Implemented in Lesson 2.3

ISTE STANDARDS FOR EDUCATORS	ISTE STANDARDS FOR STUDENTS	CONTENT AREA STANDARDS
Citizen 3b, 3c Designer 5b Facilitator 6a, 6d Analyst 7a	Digital Citizen 2c Knowledge Constructor 3a Innovative Designer 4c Creative Communicator 6b, 6c, 6d Global Collaborator 7c	Students will engage in math geometry standards and standards of mathematical practice, while practicing speaking and learning skills.

Instructions

Explain the Jigsaw presentation method to students and provide some examples of short mini-lessons they can use. For example, students may create a short video, write a song or rap, display or provide an infographic poster, or teach a live interactive lesson. Explain that they will work with their groups to create a 3–4 minute mini-lesson that they will teach to the rest of the class. Students can use their textbooks, YouTube or Khan Academy videos, and other presentations to help learn their content. When explaining this process to students, stress the importance of creating a lesson they feel will help students develop a better understanding of the content. Provide students with the Math Jigsaw Rubric.

Provide 5–10 minutes for students to brainstorm lesson ideas with their groups. Stress that this time is for brainstorming ideas, not beginning their lessons or materials.

Provide students 45–60 minutes to create their lesson. They will need to make two copies of everything in their presentation, as some members of the team will stay at their desks (home team), and others will travel from group to group (traveling team). If working online, students can use an online document to collaborate and curate their research.

Provide students with time to practice their presentations and select the home and traveling team members. Ideally, you would have two home team members and two travelers, but there are variations for this. Review the Jigsaw procedures with students, how the home team will stay at their desks as the travelers move each round. I use an interval timer (see Chapter 6 for more details) to help manage the time for each round. Additionally, I remind students that the guests share first, and then the home team. Each round should last 5–8 minutes, depending on the length of their presentations.

Between each round, provide groups 1–2 minutes to take notes. They will be using these later. After all the rounds are complete, ask students to return to their original groups. This is the most important part of the lesson. Students will relay the information they learned and compare notes. They will discuss the similarities between the concepts shared and discuss how the concepts build on each other and how they can be applied in authentic life situations.

Extensions

One extension is to allow students to post their mini-lessons on a website or online platform to be shared with other classes. Additionally, it may be possible to add some of these lessons to your district curriculum maps.

ONLINE AND REMOTE LEARNING ADAPTATION

Explain the math jigsaw presentations and assign topics during a synchronous videoconference session. Next, students will collaborate using Google Docs or Microsoft Word online, and, if possible, use videoconference breakout rooms or an online discussion to share ideas. They will conduct research and complete their mini-lessons to align with the Jigsaw rubric. Students will present their Jigsaw presentations using Flipgrid, Seesaw, their LMS, or another video hosting platform.

LESSON PLAN 2.4 Student-Created Tutorial Videos

Subject: Any content area

Target Grades: K–12

Duration: 60–90 minutes

I have yet to meet a student who does not love YouTube videos, and many are excited at the prospect of creating their own. Although it may not be possible to ask students to create their own channel and begin creating tutorials (especially if your students are under 13), there are ways to encourage a variation of this in your own classroom. Along with promoting presentation and public speaking skills, this lesson gives students the opportunity to become an expert in something or tell their story.

This lesson uses Flipgrid (**info.flipgrid.com**) for engaging students in video creation. A free tool, Flipgrid allows teachers to create grids in which students can easily create and post their videos, and provide feedback on their classmates' videos. Similarly, Padlet (**padlet.com**) is a freemium product that also allows students to create and upload videos to a shared wall and add comments. Teachers with a free account can create three walls but would need to purchase a pro account to add more. With both of these tools, students learn valuable digital citizenship skills, including how to brand and promote themselves in an appropriate way. As with YouTube, teachers can allow students to like and comment on videos, creating authentic feedback and increasing their sense of purpose.

Objectives

Grades K–12 students will be able to:

+ Demonstrate their knowledge of content standards and topics while practicing communication skills.

+ Explain concepts in a clear and concise way.

+ Adapt their videos to meet the needs of their audience.

+ Use content vocabulary words correctly in context.

Preparation

Materials:

+ Video Creation Tool (Flipgrid, Padlet, iMovie, Clips, WeVideo, or similar)

+ Optional: Dry-erase blank photo booth speech bubbles or dry-erase boards

+ Optional: Dry-erase markers

+ Optional: Headsets with microphones

Advanced Preparation:

+ Create a photobooth station.

+ Create a Flipgrid topic board.

Standards Implemented in Lesson 2.4

ISTE STANDARDS FOR EDUCATORS	ISTE STANDARDS FOR STUDENTS	CONTENT AREA STANDARDS
Citizen 3c Designer 5b Facilitator 6a, 6d Analyst 7a	Digital Citizen 2c Creative Communicator 6b, 6c, 6d Global Collaborator 7c	Students will engage in an authentic assessment of content standards, while using vocabulary words in context. Students will also practice speaking and listening skills.

Instructions

 When introducing this project to students, show some examples of tutorial videos. Ask students to explain what they notice: What are the features of a tutorial video? What made it effective? Write their responses on a shared guide or chart paper as you begin creating guidelines for their videos. For middle- and high-school classrooms, you could introduce students to multimedia principles and include those in the rubric as well.

 Demonstrate how students will create their videos. This can be individually or in small groups. With younger students, I recommend beginning with partners and moving toward larger groups as they practice collaboration.

 I recommend having students create their videos during small group instruction and station rotations, if possible. This will reduce background noise. You can set up a photobooth station with interchangeable Velcro backgrounds and photobooth props. Alternatively, students can wear headsets with microphones. Secondary students can complete videos in class, or at home as a homework assignment.

 When students visit the photobooth station, they will write their vocabulary words on the photobooth props, practice their video, and then record. Optional: Students will edit their videos, adding title slides, effects, and music.

 Students can submit their videos in a variety of ways: Flipgrid, Padlet, an LMS discussion board, Google Drive, or OneDrive.

  During the next station rotation, provide opportunities for students to watch other videos and reflect on what they learned. You can also provide opportunities to peer review other videos before publishing them online.

Extensions

Students can share their tutorials with other classes—for example, with younger students or students in classes around the world. The teacher can create a website to feature student work and invite other classes to visit and learn.

ONLINE AND REMOTE LEARNING ADAPTATION

In an online classroom, students can use tools such as Flipgrid or Seesaw to create their tutorial videos. They can submit their videos on those platforms for classmates to either peer review or watch and learn.

COACH'S CONNECTION

Edtech coaches take on many roles: collaborator, course creator, trainer, marketer, and more. Chapter 2 discusses the importance of design in our world, and how multimedia principles can be introduced to students when implementing projects. Our role as an instructional designer provides a unique opportunity to model research-based principles and strategies for our teachers. Specifically, the Learning Designer standard states that "coaches model the use of instructional design principles with educators to create effective digital learning environments" (ISTE Standards for Coaches, 4d, 2019). To support your efforts to meet this standard, the sections that follow will provide an overview of some of my favorite resources to help design online and blended courses for educators.

Instructional Design Models

It can be challenging to create a course or professional learning event that meets the needs of all participants. Two resources that will help you ensure that your courses are ADA compliant, free of bias, well-designed, and include strong instructional elements are the standards documents available from the Aurora Institute and Quality Matters:

✦ iNACOL National Standards for Quality Online Courses. The Aurora Institute (formerly the International Association for K–12 Online Learning or iNACOL) provides a comprehensive set of standards that includes academic elements such as providing a clear course overview, as well as elements to remind designers to include acceptable use policies, copyright expectations, and privacy policies. Additionally, these standards include a rubric that addresses instructional design elements, technology use, and accessibility features. I use this rubric for evaluating my courses, and I feel it would be extremely beneficial to use during peer reviews as well. Evaluating courses using the objective lens of a rubric is a time-consuming process, but I feel more confident in my course after doing so. To download the standards document, visit **bit.ly/31xAisy**.

- QM Course Design Rubric Standards. Quality Matters provides online course rubrics for higher education and K–12 designers. The K–12 rubric (**bit.ly/39wJNLX**) offers some elements that are missing from the iNACOL rubric. For example, student confidentiality is addressed in the Course Technology section of the Quality Matters rubric. This rubric is less comprehensive, making it a good option for courses that will only be offered once or twice, or when you are designing a course within a short time-span.

Evaluating Instructional Resources with Mayer's Principles

Whether you're evaluating student presentations, a teacher's instructional resources, or a textbook, Mayer's Principles of Multimedia Learning (2008) can be beneficial. These principles outline research-based best practices, thereby providing stronger reasoning for your feedback than simply stating something like, "This layout will be challenging for students." In addition to those discussed earlier in the chapter, some of Mayer's principles that are relevant when evaluating content are:

- Spatial Contiguity Principle. This principle states that people learn better when corresponding words and pictures are presented near, rather than far, from each other on a page or screen. For example, a poorly designed online reading comprehension assessment might place the reading passage on pages 1 and 2, and the corresponding questions on pages 3 through 6, requiring students to click back through the pages to consult the text, then click forward again to provide their answer. A better design would be to include the text on each page of questions for easier reference.

- Redundancy Principle. Very similar to the design tip for students, "You are giving a presentation, not a document," this principle states that onscreen text along with audio narration and graphics make it more difficult to retain content. It is more beneficial to include audio narration and graphics rather than onscreen text. Not only can you apply this principle when evaluating video content but also when creating your own tutorial videos. (I still catch myself reading text on a slide in my videos at times.) For example, consider turning off closed captions in videos, unless you have hearing-impaired participants in your session.

+ Temporal Contiguity Principle. This principle encourages designers to present graphics and their corresponding text simultaneously, rather than one after the other. Slideshow presentations often include animations that can be distracting and increase cognitive load if they are not displayed in conjunction with accompanying text. This issue is not as common in videos, but it is something to look out for when evaluating instructional materials.

+ Pre-training Principle. Often ignored when teachers are rushing to cover material in their courses, this principle states that students learn better when information is frontloaded with vocabulary and key concepts prior to the lesson. This reminds me of Bloom's Taxonomy and Webb's Depth of Knowledge, in which the lower levels call for recall of knowledge and basic facts before applying, creating, or synthesizing that information. This is something to think about when modeling lessons. As a coach, I do not always have time to cover content in my lessons as I would in a class with my own students. One solution for this is to provide the teacher with key concepts and vocabulary to address prior to your lesson, or you can select lessons that review content students already learned in class.

+ Voice Principle. Especially useful when evaluating textbook and instructional materials, this principle states that people learn better when a human voice, rather than a machine or computer, provides the content. Often publishers offer audio narration for assessments and other content as the result of text-to-speech conversion, rather than a human voice. Finding and using resources that follow the Voice Principle can go a long way toward helping students understand the information they are viewing.

If you are a coach and have not had the opportunity to evaluate digital textbooks yet, I recommend offering your support for this type of project. Doing so will help you get to know the textbooks, while also providing an opportunity to explore features and address any potential concerns prior to purchasing the product. When my colleagues and I evaluate digital textbooks, I apply Mayer's Principles of Multimedia Learning while looking for usability and accessibility resources such as assessments with audio support, and technology glitches. The process typically takes one to three hours per textbook, as you log in to the publisher's site as a teacher to assign materials, then as a student to test materials, and again as an administrator to view reports.

Purposeful Digital Citizenship

Although digital citizenship has been a hot topic for years, it is constantly evolving and definitely not yet mastered by most students—or many adults, for that matter. To that end, the ISTE Standards for Coaches call on us to become Digital Citizen Advocates by "partnering with educators, leaders, students and families to foster a culture of respectful online interactions and a healthy balance in their use of technology" and "supporting educators and students to critically examine the sources of online media and identify underlying assumptions" (7b and 7c, 2019). One way you can do this is to help teachers understand how many ways they can embed digital citizenship in their daily lessons and projects without taking up too much time or interfering with their pacing guides.

One way to incorporate digital citizenship into your model lessons and professional learning sessions is to clone yourself—digitally, at least. Enlisting an avatar or other online character, or even other students, to point out privacy and safety issues is a good way to get the message across without students feeling like their teacher is nagging them. When I taught second grade, for example, I created a talking dog with Voki (**voki.com**) to join our blog to point out positive student behaviors, while also reminding students not to post their personal information (Figure 2.1). In a secondary classroom, you could choose a student to act as the avatar or mascot, and then trade out students daily or weekly. For your model lessons, you could create an avatar or mascot when using online discussion platforms such as Padlet (**padlet.com**), Blogger (**blogger.com**), or Seesaw (**web.seesaw.me**). This can be trickier in a district-managed LMS, unless you are able to add users. If so, you could add one account that all coaches could share. Avatars can be as simple or dramatic as you like. You can also provide awards or badges from your digital citizenship pal. Online discussions and projects offer many opportunities for students to post comments online, as well as a small opportunity to address privacy, safety, and online etiquette without taking time with additional lessons.

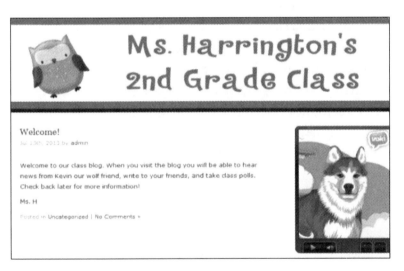

2.1 For my second-grade class, I used a talking avatar to remind students not to share personal information and how to comment kindly.

Another important aspect of digital citizenship for teachers, parents, and other stakeholders in your school district to understand is the difference between active and passive uses of technology. *Passive technology use* consists of students viewing content, not interacting with the technology, or having no choices related to the use. Watching a YouTube video is a prime example of passive technology use. *Active technology use* provides students with opportunities to explore, create, remix, collaborate, and make their own choices. Creating a stop-motion video is an active use of technology.

In 2017, the U.S. Department of Education released a report with guidelines for technology use in a K–3 classroom, including:

+ Children ages 2–5: One hour of screen time per day is appropriate.
+ Children ages 6–8: Technology should be used as a tool for children to explore and become creators.

The report also conceded that more research on screen time is needed, specifically to distinguish between active and passive technology use.

As a coach, you have several opportunities to share this information with stakeholders in your school or district. During professional learning training and courses, provide examples of passive and active use, for example, and include active technology use in rubrics for any lesson plans required during your training. During sessions, teachers can work cooperatively to create examples of active technology activities to include in their lessons. Additionally, you can host or attend parent events, providing them with information about the difference between passive and active technology use. Here are a few other ways you can promote digital citizenship across your school or district:

+ Provide task cards with home technology challenges that parents and students can complete together. For example, families can create a video in iMovie or Clips to share what they eat for dinner. Another task could be to create a family podcast, asking questions about their family tree and discussing their traditions. As incentive, families completing challenges could earn prizes or points in a classroom competition. For example, each student in a class who completes the challenge with their family earns a point for the class. For students with families who are unable to participate, teachers can pair them with a mentor or older student to complete the task. Students can draw a picture of what they eat for dinner or their traditions and create a voice-over to explain. Then the class with the most points wins a popcorn and movie party. Or you can make the goal achievable by each class, stating that any class with 80% of students completing the challenge will earn the reward.

+ Model healthy screen time usage. Coaches can help teachers model healthy screen time usage, with some simple apps and browser add-ons. One of my favorite Chrome add-ons is Take A Break by Eye Care Plus. This program reminds you to take breaks from the screen at regular intervals, which helps both reduce eyestrain and increase productivity. There is an abundance of evidence to show that taking breaks actually helps students and employees perform more efficiently, make fewer mistakes, and develop better solutions to problems (Steinborn and Huestegge, 2016). iPhones, iPads, and mobile Android devices also contain screen time features, which allow users to track usage and restrict the time spent on the device or in certain types of apps.

+ Promote technology use awareness. Encourage teachers to analyze their usage, set goals, and inspire their students to do the same. As a coach, you can also lead initiatives that call on teachers and students to ditch their devices for a certain period of time, later reflecting on how it went and embracing opportunities to explore nature and participate in hands-on learning experiences.

+ Check out the Media Balance lessons on Common Sense Media (**bit.ly/3eVUOru**). These provide opportunities for students to reflect on their current screen time use and set goals to reduce the amount of time they spend on a device. If you have opportunities to lead digital citizenship sessions with students, these are an excellent resource.

+ Assist teachers and students with using Creative Commons to protect their work. You can visit **creativecommons.org** to learn more and get started. Again, modeling is key, so if teachers are protecting their work, students may notice this and be more likely to do this themselves.

Use the hashtag #AuthenticEdVentures to share how you are using the strategies and lessons in this chapter. I would love to hear other ideas for how you are providing opportunities for students to use Mayer's Principles of Multimedia Learning and how you are encouraging students to practice their presentations.

CHAPTER 3

COLLABORATE FOR SUCCESS

Integrating student-centered projects in the classroom can be extremely rewarding; most of my favorite teaching moments come from these types of lessons, in fact. At the same time, however, project-based lessons can be extremely time-consuming and overwhelming during the planning phase. For example, creating a list of copyright-friendly photo resources takes up time that could be spent designing engaging mini-lessons to accompany a project. As educators, we encourage students to work together during projects, yet often feel like we need to be a superhero and go it alone during the planning phase. You don't have to! Collaborating and sharing resources with other educators will help decrease the amount of time you spend creating tedious rubrics, project outlines, and reflection documents. These collaborations can also increase the time you have to brainstorm creative ideas, provide feedback for your students' work, and check in with students on the status of current projects. Basically, by crowdsourcing the project planning with your personal learning network (PLN), you can free up time to spend on what really matters: your students.

Back in the early days of my career, connecting with other educators beyond my school walls was difficult. Crowdsourcing wasn't yet common, Pinterest was years from launching, and Twitter had only just appeared. Now, though, we can easily reach out to a plethora of resources and online friends ready to talk through ideas with us and share their expertise and resources. ISTE recognizes the benefits of sharing beyond the bubble of a school or district, encouraging us to "dedicate planning time to collaborate with colleagues to create authentic learning experiences that leverage technology" (ISTE Standards for Educators, Collaborator 4a, 2017). The potential rewards that come as we build these channels of communication among global educators affect not only us but also our students. Modeling these connections with students helps them see the benefits of networking and building their own PLNs, of collaborating in the classroom and beyond. To that end, this chapter explores ways to leverage the network of educators in your PLN and collaborate effectively. Additionally, we will explore student collaboration methods, including peer review, authentic audience members, expert videoconferences, and global collaboration.

Some Lesser-Known Educator Sharing Tools

Pinterest, Twitter chats, and TeachersPayTeachers are all excellent resources for connecting with other educators, but if we stay only on the well-established paths, we see only what everyone else sees. Take a step beyond "the usual," and try some of these lesser-known resources that are great for reaching out to and sharing ideas with other educators:

+ Voxer. A walkie-talkie type app, Voxer (**voxer.com**) allows users to send audio messages back and forth. You can communicate with one friend or in a larger chat room with many colleagues. Educators quickly recognized the value of this app, creating topic rooms for a multitude of educational subjects, which serve as less-public venues for educators to tackle challenging questions and issues they are facing. The EdSquad curates a list of Voxer chats and educators at **theedsquad.org/voxer**.

+ Facebook Live. Calling Facebook "lesser-known" may seem odd, but does it come to mind when you hear "education resource?" It should. Numerous educators use Facebook Live (**live.fb.com**) to share their favorite tips and provide small tours of their classrooms. Again, there are educational Facebook groups for nearly any program or app, as well as some to explore topics such as virtual reality, social-emotional learning, and many others. Facebook has a list of many of these groups, which can be found at **bit.ly/2XhiC31**. Live video is fun, as you never know what will happen, often making it more interesting than professionally edited videos that typically show only the polished version of a lesson.

+ Feedly. The Feedly platform (**feedly.com**) allows you to curate collections of blogs and websites that you can peruse each day. Rather than visiting numerous websites and blogs to find resources, you can simply use Feedly, which maintains everything in one place. I typically check it once or twice per week, and I am able to keep up with all the educators I follow. Feedly also allows educators to bookmark resources to save and revisit. This helps coaches support other coaches and techy educators, while staying current on the latest tools and strategies.

ENHANCE PROJECTS WITH CONTENT EXPERTS

Along with sharing project resources, our PLNs can help us locate guest experts to serve as guides to students during projects. It can be as simple as phoning a friend. For instance, reach out to your school's media specialists, instructional and edtech coaches, or STEM teachers to ask if they'd be willing to help facilitate and organize your project. These experts typically welcome any opportunity to work with students, and having an extra set of hands can be helpful. Students also benefit from hearing a variety of voices and learning unique perspectives and ideas. This is also a great way to model collaboration and show students how adults work together to support a common goal. Most projects incorporate some type of research, so including your media specialists is a natural fit. Media specialists are often able to provide lessons on effective and reliable searches. They are also typically experts in digital citizenship and can help explain copyright and fair use guidelines with students. Instructional coaches and Special Education teachers are helpful with scaffolding information for students who need extra support.

Beyond Face-To-Face Guest Speakers

Depending on the project, your students could also benefit from the assistance of authors, engineers, marketing professionals, and others who are willing to share their knowledge. A classroom exchange with an expert typically includes a presentation from the speaker, along with time for students to interact with them and ask questions. If the expert can't visit your classroom in person, perhaps they could virtually through videoconferencing. Not only does this enable your students to hear from and discuss projects with distant experts, but it is also a great opportunity to increase cultural diversity in your classroom. Let students see that anyone can become a writer, game designer, or historian. University of Florida research demonstrated that engagement is better when students are able to learn from someone of their same race and gender. Even an hour learning from someone who looks like them can make a world of difference (Spence, 2019). What a gift we can give our students by allowing them to engage with professionals who look like them and can inspire them in ways that we cannot.

How do you connect with professionals to meet your class face-to-face or online? Try reaching out to your local universities for a start. Many PhD students and professors are eager to connect with classrooms and participate in ongoing projects. In my home state, for example, University of Florida's Thompson Earth Systems Institute offers a program called "Scientist in Every Florida School" that seeks "to build long-term collaborative relationships between teachers and scientists" (Thompson Earth Systems Institute, 2020). Another great resource, Skype in the Classroom (see the "Videoconferencing Tools" sidebar) maintains the most comprehensive list I have found for connecting students with professionals: authors, biologists, doctors, historians, and more—even a monorail driver. For technology professionals, Code.org maintains a database of computer scientists who are willing to connect with classrooms. Visit **code.org/volunteer** to find one in your area or book a virtual exchange. Finally, you could try a paid website, such as Nepris (**nepris.com**) and FieldTripZoom (**fieldtripzoom.com**) to find a guest speaker. However, I have been able to find the connections I need through free sites and quick shout-outs to my PLN.

Another alternative is to let your students take the lead. While implementing a project, why not encourage your students to reach out to experts—and practice writing skills at the same time? If you decide to do this, I recommend using a platform that allows you to moderate all communication. This ensures that your students are protected and unable to share personal information, such as their home address. Initially, students can write a letter, and later connect with the experts using a tool such as Flipgrid (**info.flipgrid.com**) or Padlet (**padlet.com**), which enables you to moderate and monitor all communication.

Tips for Successful Guest Speaker Exchanges

Guest speaker events can be exciting and memorable for students, but they can also be full of pitfalls and stress for you as a facilitator. I recently facilitated a session with an author for an elementary class in which her screen kept freezing. Students thought this was hilarious, but she didn't understand why they were laughing. Technology issues like this are not uncommon, so to ensure a smooth running day (or at least fewer headaches), here are a few tips:

Check your school or district policy pertaining to student videoconferencing. You may need to engage in videoconferencing as a class using your teacher computer, for example. Knowing the policy before you begin helps not only ensure a smooth session but also that you'll be allowed to book subsequent professionals as speakers and mentors for your class.

+ Provide the speaker a list of guidelines. Remind them about the amount of time they have to speak and about your project or unit goals. Encourage them to use visuals in their presentations and make it interactive. You can also help them prepare by providing them with a short description of your students. For example, if you are hosting a guest speaker for a class of students with autism, it is important for the speaker to understand their communication style and need for a routine and schedule.

+ Hardwire your technology. If you use an Apple TV or other screencast device, this might be a time to plug in with an HDMI or other cable instead, to ensure that you have the most stable connection possible. It is preferable that you hardwire with an Ethernet cable to the computer you will be using for the exchange, rather than relying on a Wi-Fi network. Reach out to your school's tech support specialist to see if they are available to help with your exchange. If not, ask if they can help you get set up ahead of time.

+ Have a Plan B ready. Whenever humans and technology are involved in anything, it is wise to have a Plan B. For classroom exchanges, you will need to have an engaging backup plan ready in case you are unable to connect or your guest speaker cancels. For instance, as Plan B you could ask students to view the speaker's website or articles the speaker wrote to research answers to the questions they had prepared. Students can share these on a Padlet wall or other digital discussion board. Students can also write their questions and use a tool such as Flipgrid to send them to the speaker, who will respond when they are able. With younger students, I use Google Earth when exchanges are cancelled, allowing them to take a virtual tour to the guest speaker's location.

Provide an Authentic Audience

Just as hearing from guest speakers and content experts can benefit students, having these same guests hear *them* can increase their self-regulation and build confidence in skills related to their project. For this reason and more, access to authentic audience members for students as they create and publish their projects is part of the Gold Standard PBL model (PBLWorks, 2020). An authentic, public audience can take many forms, and some authentic audience members may be closer to home than you realize.

Typically, when we think about inviting an "authentic audience" into our classroom, it can sound like a daunting task full of online research, scheduling, and extensive conversations. For many school projects, however, students can present their content to experts within their own school walls, many of whom are not typically provided opportunities to engage with students in this type of way. Consider including school administrators, custodians, cafeteria staff, and other staff members or volunteers. Most non-instructional staff are pulled in many directions and spend little time truly engaging with students and seeing the results of their contributions. Allowing them to visit the classroom and participate in projects benefits them just as much as your students.

VIDEOCONFERENCING TOOLS

When students collaborate with "visiting" experts or peers in classrooms across the globe through videoconferencing, the technology almost becomes invisible as the learning and connections take the focus. Despite this disappearing act, videoconferencing tools are some of the most valuable technology tools you can add to your classroom. They provide students with opportunities to hear from and collaborate with content experts and cultures they might never encounter otherwise. Likewise, virtual collaborations can help you expand and deepen the connections in your personal learning network, as well as provide learning and growth opportunities as you exchange ideas with distant peers. Here are three popular and free videoconference tools for classrooms:

➤ Skype in the Classroom (**education.skype.com**) is used by educators all over the world. The platform helps teachers and coaches connect with guest speakers, find virtual field trips, and connect with other classrooms. I recommend Skype in the Classroom if you are looking for professionals to connect with, as I have found their expert list to be the most comprehensive of any platform I've used.

➤ Google Meet (**meet.google.com**) is the simplest tool of the three. It includes a chat feature and the ability to screen share, and it is a good choice if students are leading the videoconference independently, as there are fewer "rabbit holes" for them to follow.

➤ Zoom (**zoom.us/education**) supports up to 100 people in a video call, as well as such custom features as polling, screen sharing, whiteboard capabilities, and breakout rooms. Students love expressing their style and interests by adding a virtual background to their video. Zoom allows the teacher to customize features for each videoconference, such as disabling the chat or restricting students from talking. This is helpful when determining the level of interactivity you would like students to have with each speaker.

In addition, check your district or school learning management system; most use some type of videoconference tool. For example, Schoology uses a platform called BigBlueButton that integrates with its management system.

I recommend becoming well-versed in these main platforms so you are able to adapt and provide flexibility to those who may not be as tech-savvy. Usually, your guest speakers and classrooms will want to use the platform with which they feel most comfortable.

Extending your audience beyond your classroom walls or community is also easy and an important step in helping students become Global Collaborators, which the ISTE Standards for Students describe as students who "use digital tools to broaden their perspectives and enrich their learning by collaborating with others and working effectively in teams locally and globally" (2016). Many teachers are willing to connect their classes with your students, and a variety of tools and programs exist to locate and connect willing classrooms. Here are a few of my favorites:

✦ Empatico. Devoted to cultivating an empathetic future generation with a greater understanding of others around the world, Empatico (**empatico.org**) is a free tool for connecting classrooms of 6- to 11-year-olds. Simply register your class, listing your grade level and availability, and Empatico will locate available matching classrooms from around the world. Further, the site provides lesson plans and guidelines to make the transition to videoconferencing easy for teachers and students. Empatico also offers seasonal projects, such as STEMpatico, that combine professional development and student learning. In collaboration with Cisco, STEMpatico provides teachers with professional learning opportunities to help encourage empathy while students participate in design thinking and STEM projects.

✦ TeachSDGs. The TeachSDGs organization (**teachsdgs.org**) is dedicated to teaching the United Nations Sustainable Development Goals (SDGs) in K–12 classrooms. Including such goals as Climate Action and Gender Equality, the SDGs were developed in an effort to transform our world for the better by the year 2030. The #TeachSDGs movement has encouraged thousands of students to take action and participate in shared projects that inspire change, ranging from public service announcements to inventions. If you are interested in participating, visit **worldslargestlesson.globalgoals.org**, which features free lesson plans and resources to support each SDG goal. Additionally, TeachSDGs offers valuable lessons and connects educators with SDG ambassadors who serve as mentors.

- Flipgrid GridPals. GridPals (**blog.flipgrid.com/news/gridpals**) is an initiative that educators using Flipgrid can turn on with the click of a button. GridPals provides access to projects created by teachers around the world. Create and post your own projects and invite other educators to participate in your shared grid, connecting students through video.

- Skype in the Classroom. In addition to being a great source for finding guest speakers, Skype in the Classroom also enables you to connect your students with other classrooms around the globe. The Mystery Skype program (**education.skype.com/p/notes**) pairs classes to guess each other's location or guess a mystery number or animal. This program is a great way to prepare students for the public speaking and problem solving involved in most projects.

Practicing diverse types of communication with their peers will help students become more skilled at interacting with others, progressing from being awkward, nervous, and quiet to valuing the opportunity to connect online and confidently speak their ideas or ask questions. Remember, it takes practice for students to become skilled at this, so providing a multitude of opportunities will build their confidence and comfort with using collaboration tools and communicating in unique ways. If these types of projects interest you, I recommend the book *Teach Boldly: Using Edtech for Social Good* by Dr. Jennifer Williams (iste.org/TeachBoldly). Her inspiring book provides detailed steps to help you engage students in collaborative global projects.

ENGAGING STUDENTS IN PEER REVIEW

One vital communication skill that will benefit students in collaborative projects—whether in the classroom, online, or their future careers—is the ability to provide and respond to peer review. Peer review is a powerful tool that helps encourage reflection and self-regulation, while building student confidence in their writing and other academic skills. Peer review is particularly beneficial for collaborative projects, as student reviewers are more invested in the outcome, leading to thoughtful feedback. For example, if one group member designs a flyer, their teammates are invested and want to ensure that the text makes sense and is error-free. Peer-review strategies are not only useful for creating high-quality products; they are also a great way to practice indicator 7b of the Global Collaborator standard, which states, "students use collaborative technologies to work with others, including peers, experts or community members, to examine issues and problems from multiple viewpoints" (ISTE Standards for Students, 7b, 2016).

Peer-Review Benefits

Boud, Cohen, and Sampson conducted research and found several benefits of the peer-review strategy. One is that peer review helps students feel more comfortable giving and receiving feedback, as well as helping to self-regulate their learning (2014). Think of a time when you experienced something and then wondered how your own project, art, movement, or the like compared. This happens both when we experience something wonderful, as well as when we experience something that is not up to par. Further, Boud, Cohen, and Sampson found that students learn more from people at their own level of learning (2014). This makes a great case for peer review and also prompts educators to create homogenous groups during collaborative projects.

Watson found that peer review is better suited for an online environment. Students provide more honest and conscientious feedback when provided more time for reflection and when engaging in an online versus face-to-face conversation (2008). In addition to this research, Wisniewski, Zierer, and Hattie listed feedback as one of the top ten influences on student achievers

(2020). Some ways to ensure that students are receiving the most effective, high-quality feedback from their peers are:

+ Train your students. Your students need to be taught what constitutes quality feedback and that "Great job!" is not sufficient. Before my students engage in peer review, I recommend modeling the process with students: Display a piece of student writing, provide a constructive compliment, and then ask students to do the same. When a student offers a comment such as "great job," ask them if they feel this is specific feedback that will help the writer improve. Discuss this each time students suggest general feedback, as well as what more specific feedback they might offer instead. One strategy for younger students is to ask them to provide two compliments and one critique. With older students, challenge them to ask questions rather than offering feedback, for example: "Do you feel that your writing flows when you read it out loud? How can you use sentence fluency to help with this?" ReadWriteThink (2003) expands on this with the Praise, Question, Polish strategy of peer review. You can locate their Narrative PQP Peer-Review Form at **bit.ly/39LWDX9**.

+ Include a rubric. Similar to their use with projects, rubrics assist students in meeting expectations during the peer-review process. For older students, I ask peer reviewers to use the same rubric I will use to grade their papers. For K–2 students, you could include prompts or stickers that represent comments. If a student's writing is detailed and descriptive, students could place a sticker of a picture frame. The picture frame represents how descriptive writing creates a visual image in the reader's brain. Younger students can use paper and pencil to peer review but then snap a picture to post online. Technology is not always the best answer, and using stickers may help engage your students in the peer-review process.

+ Provide opportunities to reflect on feedback. Providing and receiving feedback are only the beginning of the review and revision process. Students need time to reflect on the feedback they've received, whether through journal writing, student-teacher conferencing, or student-created videos. Reflection is often neglected due to time constraints, but it is the most important step in this process. To increase self-regulation, ask students to reflect on how (or if) they plan to make changes to their own paper based on their peer reviews.

Types of Peer Review

There are many ways to initiate peer review in your classroom, depending on the grade level, ability, and interest of your students. Here are three ways to get you started:

+ Multi-Student Peer Review. Students post their work on a website or document that is accessible to all students. Students provide feedback to two or more of their peers. Additionally, students can use other students' feedback as examples, to serve as scaffolding for those struggling. The downside is that all students will be able to see the feedback and could potentially copy responses. I find this type of peer review works well in primary classrooms, where students are more comfortable with others viewing their work.

+ Partner Peer Review. This is more likely what came to mind when you considered the peer-review process. Students are paired, and each reviews their partner's work, providing feedback. This method is more private and more comfortable for students who are reluctant to display their work. With some technology programs, you can even arrange for both student work and reviews to appear anonymously.

+ Mixed Methods Peer Review. Another option is to incorporate these two strategies in a tiered peer-review process. Students are partnered during the first round of revisions, then make revisions and post their second draft for the entire class to critique.

Peer Review Tools

Although students can certainly provide feedback to their peers using pen and paper, by employing digital tools they can also apply indicator 1c of the Empowered Learner standard, which states that "students use technology to seek feedback that informs and improves their practice and to demonstrate their learning in a variety of ways" (ISTE Standards for Students, 1c, 2016). Here are some of my favorite tools, most of which are simple enough for even your youngest learners to use:

✦ Buncee. Although a paid program, Buncee (**app.edu.buncee.com**) is my top choice for multi-student peer review, especially with younger students. This program allows students to record audio over their slides and post their presentations on a Buncee board (a digital bulletin board) for other students to watch and provide comments.

✦ Padlet. Like a digital bulletin board, Padlet (**padlet.com**) allows students to post their presentations or projects on a shared wall. They can also upload pictures, audio, and video files. Other students can comment to add feedback. A free account allows teachers to create three boards. Padlet is a good option for multi-student peer review.

✦ Classkick. Available in free and paid versions, Classkick (**classkick.com**) enables students to write, type, and draw while the teacher can monitor students as they work live. My favorite optional feature is how Classkick allows students to anonymously help each other and provide comments. For example, a message will pop up on a student's screen as "Helpful Hare gave you a suggestion." Helpful Hare is actually one of their randomly selected classmates. The talking avatar feature makes Classkick very kid-friendly and a great collaboration tool.

✦ Google Workspace (formerly G Suite). Comprised of Google Docs, Slides, and Sheets, Google Workspace/G Suite (**edu.google.com/products /gsuite-for-education**) allows students to collaborate to edit documents in real time. My favorite feature is the version history, which enables students and teachers to review individual contributions and restore the document to previous versions if a student deletes their partner's work or makes a mistake that alters the document. Google Workspace is a great option for partner peer review.

+ Canvas. If your school or district uses the Canvas LMS (**instructure.com /canvas**), you can take advantage of its peer-review feature for assignments. I frequently use this with my college students. Students can be manually or automatically paired with a partner who will review their work. You can also choose to make peer reviews anonymous.

As with most other skills associated with projects and PBL, peer review will take time to perfect. Students need modeling, training, and practice to become better at giving and receiving constructive reviews. The following lesson plans will help you get them started.

LESSON PLANS

As you read through the lesson plans, consider how these projects are strengthened by the inclusion of an authentic audience, guest experts, and peer review. These examples can also help you make adjustments to your existing projects to provide students with unique perspectives and opportunities to connect with others globally.

LESSON PLAN 3.1 Algorithmic Thinking Project

Subject: Math/Entrepreneurship

Target Grades: 6–12

Duration: 3–4 class periods

Students will have the opportunity to become entrepreneurs as they explore math concepts and algorithmic thinking. They will interview school staff members (teachers, cafeteria managers, maintenance workers, administrators, etc.), and determine problems and challenges they are facing due to lack of efficiency and automation. Next, each group of students will select one problem to solve. They will use spreadsheets or coding programs to automate tasks and help school members solve their problem more efficiently and effectively.

Objectives

Grades 6–12 students will be able to:

+ Recognize how to make tasks more efficient through automation.
+ Design their own algorithms in order to solve problems.
+ Test their algorithms for bugs and revise their prototype.
+ Train others on using their algorithm.

Standards Implemented in Lesson 3.1

ISTE STANDARDS FOR EDUCATORS	ISTE STANDARDS FOR STUDENTS	CONTENT AREA STANDARDS
Citizen 3a Collaborator 4b, 4c Designer 5b Facilitator 6a, 6c	Empowered Learner 1c, 1d Innovative Designer 4a, 4c, 4d Computational Thinker 5a, 5d Creative Communicator 6c, 6d Global Collaborator 7c, 7d	Students will engage in computational thinking, applying their math concepts to help solve an authentic problem. Students will engage in computer science concepts.

Preparation

Materials:

+ Spreadsheet program (Microsoft Excel, Google Sheets, Numbers, or similar)

+ Optional: Coding program (Scratch or similar)

Advanced Preparation:

+ Prepare examples of automation and algorithmic thinking.

Instructions

Show students several examples of automation and explain the meaning of the words *automation* and *algorithmic thinking*. Show several simplistic algorithms, such as a cooking recipe. Ask students to list other examples of automation and algorithmic thinking (2–3 minutes).

Explain that students will interview staff members to discuss challenges they are facing. Inform students that they will be working with their group to solve one of the identified issues by automating the task and designing an algorithm for staff members to follow. Students will use a spreadsheet program or coding platform to design algorithms that help automate common tasks. You may want students to sign up to interview specific staff members so nobody gets bombarded by multiple students.

 Split students into small groups (three or four students) and provide them time to begin brainstorming questions to help them identify challenges they can solve.

 Students email staff members to schedule interview times during the next class period. Alternately, students can create an online form using Microsoft Forms or Google Forms and distribute it to students and staff. This form includes questions to help students determine how to help employees automate their task.

 Provide time for students to conduct their interviews and begin creating plans.

 Provide time for students to develop algorithms in their spreadsheet or coding platform and begin testing them.

 Students facilitate beta testing with staff members. During this time, students should develop a survey for staff members to complete, focusing on design issues or challenges, bugs, usability, and clarity of instructions.

 Provide time for students to tweak their algorithms and/or code, addressing the issues from their customers.

Provide ways for students to publish their algorithms and begin testing with other employees, other schools, or community members.

Extensions

Students could locate leaders in their community or global leaders online and build algorithms for them. Students could focus on the career path they would like to explore and contact workers in that field.

ONLINE AND REMOTE LEARNING ADAPTATION

In an online learning environment, students can host an online form and allow teachers and staff members to submit common issues they face in their job role. Students can schedule videoconferences with individual staff members to learn more about their specific issues and/or needs. Students collaborate via videoconference tools or online discussion forums to create their algorithms, using Microsoft Excel online or Google Sheets. Students can use pair programming in Scratch, Code.org, or most other coding platforms. Pair programming is commonly used by professional programmers, and it typically involves two programmers working side by side with one writing the code while the other checks and describes it. In this adaptation, one student would create and explain the code, while the other would check the code for accuracy. Some programs allow for commenting, or students can learn how to add comments in the code. Next, students can create their algorithm or code and create a video in Flipgrid or their LMS to present their product to the teachers or staff members.

LESSON PLAN 3.2 **Pick Your Path Stories**

Subject: ELA, Science, or Social Studies

Target Grades: 3–8

Duration: 2–3 class periods

Pick Your Path stories are a way for students to have fun with writing while demonstrating their knowledge of content area topics. Teachers can incorporate research, novel studies, historical events and people, and other concepts. This project also provides students opportunities to practice logic needed for coding, with a variation on conditionals (if/else statements). This is a great opportunity for ELA and science or social studies teachers to collaborate, with students learning about concepts during their content classes and then writing the stories in English class.

Objectives

Grades 3–5 students will be able to:

✦ Write detailed narrative stories for an intended audience.

✦ Explain how they used literary elements and figurative language such as anachronism, metaphors and similes, hyperbole, and so on to make their stories more interesting.

✦ Demonstrate knowledge of content in their subject area.

Grades 6–8 students will be able to:

✦ Write detailed narrative stories for an intended audience, with attention to plot and establishing a clear point of view.

✦ Explain how they used literary elements and figurative language such as anachronism, metaphors and similes, hyperbole, and so on to make their stories more interesting.

✦ Demonstrate knowledge of content in their subject area.

Standards Implemented in Lesson 3.2

ISTE STANDARDS FOR EDUCATORS	ISTE STANDARDS FOR STUDENTS	CONTENT AREA STANDARDS
Citizen 3a, 3c Designer 5b Facilitator 6d	Knowledge Constructor 3a Creative Communicator 6d Global Collaborator 7c	Students will utilize their ELA narrative writing skills to write their stories. They will incorporate content vocabulary and information to demonstrate their knowledge of historical events, science concepts, or any other content.

Preparation

Materials:

✦ Presentation software (Google Slides, Google Forms, or similar)

✦ Optional: Pick Your Path Story Map (**bit.ly/2AVawVn**)

Advanced Preparation:

✦ Provide students with lists of online resources, along with guidelines for conducting safe and effective research.

✦ Provide students with a rubric that demonstrates the content area standards and topics that need to be included in the story.

Instructions

 Ask students about their background knowledge with Pick Your Path–style books, such as *Pick Your Quest: King Tut's Adventure* by Connor Hoover. Provide this story for students to read. Allow about 10–15 minutes for students to read and choose one adventure in the story, then write a short reflection about their experience.

 Ask students to share their experience with a partner. Discuss how their stories and endings were the same or different. Demonstrate how students will create their own stories using presentation software or Google Forms. Show how to link from slide to slide in Google Slides, for example, or to add sections in Google Forms. Be sure to practice this yourself prior to implementing this lesson for a smoother demonstration. Educator Amanda Anderson created a tutorial video you can watch at **bit.ly/3135nnG**.

 Divide students into groups to begin writing their stories on paper or in an online document. Inform students that their story will need approval prior to adding it to their slideshow. Provide students with the Pick Your Path Story Map (optional). This is also a good time to provide writing mini-lessons to review literary elements and writing techniques. You can also include videos and other resources to review the science or social studies content.

 Allow students class time to write and post their stories in your LMS, Flipgrid, or Padlet for peer reviews. Peer review is important in this lesson, as it is easy to make errors in their story maps. After incorporating corrections and suggestions from peer review, students publish their stories online. This can be a class blog, website, or other online source for their schoolmates and families to read, creating an authentic audience.

Extensions

Students can add drawings and pictures to their stories to make them more interesting. Students can use a coding platform, such as Scratch, to make their stories interactive.

ONLINE AND REMOTE LEARNING ADAPTATION

During a class videoconference, explain the project and provide examples. Provide a writing mini-lesson about literary and writing elements you would like included in the stories. Distribute the example story and provide a discussion board for students to reflect on it after reading. Create writing groups, and ask students to create a shared document using Google Docs or Microsoft Word online to brainstorm ideas for how to include the content instruction in their stories. Provide time for students to begin writing collaboratively. Lead another videoconference to distribute the Pick Your Path Story Map and explain how to create the Pick Your Path story in the platform you chose (slideshow, forms, etc.). Provide students time to work with their groups and complete the story. Students can post their completed stories in their LMS or other online platform such as Padlet or Flipgrid.

LESSON PLAN 3.3 Invent It Challenge

Subject: Science/ELA

Target Grades: K–12

Duration: 3–4 weeks

Sponsored by the Smithsonian and Cricket Media, the annual Spark!Lab Dr. InBae and Mrs. Kyung Joo Yoon Invent It Challenge features a different challenge each year, such as creating an invention to provide healthy food to everyone around the world (**inventitchallenge2020.epals.com**) or an invention that enhances daily life and activities of older adults (**inventitchallenge2019.epals.com**). Students engage in the design process as they explore their creativity and engineering skills to create an invention that helps solve a global problem (Figure 3.1).

3.1 A second-grade student designed this Popsicle holder for the 2014 Invent It Challenge.

Objectives

Grades K–12 students will be able to:

✦ Engage in the design process.

✦ Demonstrate their knowledge of science concepts while creating a realistic invention.

- Conduct research to learn more about global problems.
- Create a presentation and marketing material to help "sell" their invention.

Standards Implemented in Lesson 3.3

ISTE STANDARDS FOR EDUCATORS	ISTE STANDARDS FOR STUDENTS	CONTENT AREA STANDARDS
Citizen 3a, 3c Collaborator 4a, 4c Designer 5b Facilitator 6a Facilitator 6c, 6d	Digital Citizen 2b, 2c Knowledge Constructor 3b, 3d Innovative Designer 4a, 4b, 4c, 4d Creative Communicator 6a Global Collaborator 7b, 7c, 7d	Students will use ELA research standards and work through the engineering and design process. They will explore other science content standards such as physics, life science, and other areas specific to their invention.

Preparation

Materials:

- Spark!Lab Invent It Challenge rules and resources (**inventitchallenge2020.epals.com/how-to-enter**)
- Lists of research websites and databases

Advanced Preparation:

- Preview the Invent It Challenge website for the appropriate contest year to ensure that you understand the rules and download all the necessary materials.
- Create or locate a list of student-friendly research websites and databases.

Instructions

 Ask students what they already know about inventions. You can relate this to the *Shark Tank* TV show and bring in examples of student inventions from previous years. Ask students what they notice about each invention. Provide students with information about the current year's challenge.

 Divide students into groups and give them time to brainstorm inventions that will help solve the challenge.

 Students conduct additional research to determine if their invention will work and if anything similar has already been created. If students create an invention that already exists or is not feasible to make, begin asking them questions and providing research opportunities that will help them arrive at this conclusion themselves.

 After each group finalizes their idea, have them create a supply list of materials they need to build their prototype.

 Students work though the engineering and design process, as well as create prototypes of their invention.

 Students analyze data and begin discussions (in an LMS board or through a videoconference tool) about how to revise their prototypes.

 Students revise their prototypes based on feedback. They will create a marketing campaign for their invention. This can include podcasts, commercials, flyers, and other marketing materials. Determine which students are interested in entering the contest, obtain parent permission, and submit their inventions.

Extensions

Students can apply for patents for their invention and learn about the patent process.

ONLINE AND REMOTE LEARNING ADAPTATION

Students may need to work individually or create their own prototypes at each group member's house. Equity is also something to consider, as some students may not have the supplies needed to complete their prototype. As an alternative, you could ask students to design their invention without creating a prototype or to design their prototype using 3D printing software, such as Autodesk Tinkercad. Another option is to mail supplies to the students; however, this places extra work (and possibly financial burden) on the teacher. The fourth option is to consider projects that will be easy to create using regular household objects or materials found in nature. Students will work collaboratively using a shared online document and videoconference with team members if permitted by your school or district.

LESSON PLAN 3.4 Student-Led Citizen Science

Subject: Science/Math

Target Grades: 6–12

Duration: 1–2 weeks

Students will have the opportunity to engage in citizen science projects, which enlist the general public to help research scientists with data collection. Initially, students will participate in one or more existing projects using sources such as Zooniverse or NASA. For example, the Chimp&See project on Zooniverse tasks students with classifying animals in video footage of countries across Africa. In this particular project, scientists utilize the citizen science data to better understand chimpanzee behaviors and how they interact in their environment. After students document the research design and data collection process for the project they select, they will design their own citizen science projects and enlist the help of other students around the world.

Objectives

Grades 6–12 students will be able to:

+ Identify the methods and data in an existing citizen science project.

+ Apply science content knowledge while designing their projects.

+ Create their own citizen science project and data collection process.

+ Create a website to host their scientific research.

Preparation

Materials:

+ Citizen science websites, such as Zooniverse (**zooniverse.org**), NASA (**science.nasa.gov/citizenscience**), or National Geographic (**nationalgeographic.org/idea/citizen-science-projects**)

- Website creation platform (Google Sites, Weebly, WordPress, or similar)

- Data Collection Sheet (**bit.ly/31Yu72H**)

- Citizen Science Project Planning Sheet (**bit.ly/3e1E95k**)

- Citizen Science Project Rubric (**bit.ly/2YXFjdQ**)

Advanced Preparation:

- Preview some citizen science projects and select several that align with your course content standards.

- Locate resources for additional relevant projects so students choose one of your options or locate another project that aligns with course content.

Standards Implemented in Lesson 3.4

ISTE STANDARDS FOR EDUCATORS	ISTE STANDARDS FOR STUDENTS	CONTENT AREA STANDARDS
Leader 2a Citizen 3a, 3c Collaborator 4a, 4c Designer 5a, 5b Facilitator 6a, 6c, 6d Analyst 7a	Empowered Learner 1b, 1c Digital Citizen 2b, 2c, 2d Knowledge Constructor 3a, 3d Innovative Designer 4a, 4b, 4d Computational Thinker 5a, 5b Creative Communicator 6a, 6b, 6c, 6d Global Collaborator 7a, 7b, 7c, 7d	Students will engage in a variety of science content, as well as use the scientific process and scientific research. Students will use ELA skills such as informative writing, as well as speaking and listening skills to inform others about their citizen science project.

Instructions

Ask students what the term *citizen science* means to them. Provide 1–2 minutes for students to discuss with a partner or team. Provide a few examples of citizen science projects and ask students to determine the purpose of these projects. Why are scientists enlisting the help of citizens? Inform them that they will be creating their own citizen science projects. Provide a list of relevant citizen scientist projects from Zooniverse, NASA, or other sources.

Group students and allow them to select the project they feel is most interesting. Provide a class period for students to begin engaging in the citizen science project and recording their experience on their Data Collection Sheet. Provide an additional 15–20 minutes for students to discuss their experience with their teammates and compare data in an online discussion forum. You may want to allow students to engage in more than one project, to understand different methods they can consider when designing their own.

Distribute the Citizen Science Project Rubric and Project Planning Sheet and provide time for students to begin brainstorming their citizen science projects and how they will host their project online. If possible, secure some grant funds for this project ahead of time in case students need supplies, such as livestream or time-lapse cameras. Inform students their project could also require students to collect samples or data in their own area, allowing them to track and compare research in various locations and regions.

Provide time for students to videoconference with experts. They can ask questions to ensure that they are setting up an ethical and valid research project. Students will make changes to their plan based on the feedback they receive.

Next, students begin creating directions, their website, and any forms that will be used to collect data from their citizen scientists. Each group will create a marketing plan to recruit citizen scientists.

Students create a website with Google Sites, Weebly, or another tool and begin marketing to ensure citizen scientists are helping track data for them. Students share their projects with at least one other group and collect feedback.

Provide class time for students to check their data on a weekly or monthly basis. Students should create reports to share with the class, as well as with the citizen scientists who are helping with their research.

Extensions

Students videoconference with an expert during each step of their citizen science project. This person serves as a guide and mentor to ensure that students are using modern tools and methods to conduct their research.

ONLINE AND REMOTE LEARNING ADAPTATION

Relay directions during a videoconference call and use breakout rooms to allow groups time to discuss the citizen science projects. If breakout rooms are not possible, students can use a discussion in their LMS or in an online platform such as Padlet. Students can use a shared online document to begin planning their citizen science project and check in during videoconference calls to ensure that all teammates understand the goal of their project. You can schedule weekly videoconference check-ins with each group, to ensure that they remain focused and are creating a valid research project. When each group completes a draft project, they can post it in an LMS discussion and allow others to provide feedback.

COACH'S CONNECTION

As coaches, making connections not only allows us to gain new knowledge in our practice but also helps us connect teachers with others who have knowledge about certain topics or are interested in project collaboration. Many of the projects I initiate with teachers were brought to my attention by coaches and educators in my PLN. So where can coaches find connections?

One of the most valuable resources to me as a coach has been the International Society for Technology in Education (**istg.org**). ISTE conferences offer numerous coaching sessions, including the Edtech Coaches Playground, which is a three-hour interactive event with poster-style presentations. This playground is always packed with enthusiastic coaches sharing ideas and resources, making it my favorite part of the conference each year. A PLN meeting and other networking opportunities are always available to coaches throughout the conference. Additionally, coaches can connect through the Edtech Coaches PLN Network. This network offers forum discussions, monthly newsletters, monthly Twitter chats, and book studies. The annual ISTE Conference & Expo also includes a coaches membership meeting and several other networking events. In addition to ISTE, the Future of Education Technology Conference (FETC, **fetc.org**) offers a coaching track. Attendees can search the program to locate sessions specific for coaches.

Most states also offer an ISTE affiliate consisting of edtech leaders from across the state. Through these groups, coaches and other district leaders are able to make strong connections, receive feedback when making purchasing decisions, advocate for technology at the state and federal level, as well as organize events and meetups to share ideas and resources. While not all affiliates are alike, I highly recommend joining your affiliate and getting involved.

Facebook also offers groups to support coaches, such as the Edtech Coaches Unite PLN group and the Future Ready Instructional Coaches group.

Effective Long-Distance Collaborations and Professional Learning

The Connected Learner standard encourages edtech coaches to "pursue professional learning that deepens expertise in the ISTE Standards in order to serve as a model for educators and leaders" (ISTE Standards for Coaches, 2a, 2019). ISTE provides some avenues and resources to help coaches develop a deeper understanding of these standards:

+ ISTE U. This platform (**iste.org/learn/iste-u**) provides coaches and other educators training in the ISTE Standards and other current technology topics, such as AI in education. Although there is a fee, these online courses are taught by content experts and offer graduate credit for an additional fee.

+ ISTE Blog. With content by edtech leaders from around the world, the ISTE blog (**iste.org/explore**) regularly features posts focused on the ISTE Standards, among other topics.

Similarly, the Connected Learner standard encourages us to "actively participate in professional learning networks to enhance coaching practice and stay current with emerging technology and innovations in pedagogy and the learning sciences" (ISTE Standards for Coaches, 2b, 2019). Within my own district, opportunities are rare for coaches to attend professional learning, as we are tasked with providing our own training. For many coaches, looking beyond our schools or districts might be our only option for continuing our education and receiving training to increase our knowledge and help maintain current teaching certifications.

In addition to the opportunities afforded by an ISTE membership, you could look into massive open online courses (MOOCs) and the Future Ready Schools network (**futureready.org**). If you aren't familiar with MOOCs, they typically feature reading, videos to watch, and discussions. Once or twice a year, for example, the Friday Institute for Educational Innovation through North Carolina State offers a free MOOC to edtech coaches called Coaching Digital Learning: Cultivating a Culture of Change (**bit.ly/3cUQ9pv**). Meanwhile, the Future Ready Schools organization offers PLN networking opportunities and professional development to district leaders, including coaches.

OVERCOMING BUDGET HURDLES

Rather than finding professional learning opportunities, is your challenge getting there or funding the cost? Many budgets do not allow for educators and district leaders to attend conferences, especially for out-of-state events. Here are some tips to help you advocate for your continued learning:

➤ Share your current professional learning. When submitting a proposal to attend a conference or professional development training, describe what you currently are doing to improve your knowledge and coaching strategies. This can include books you read, Twitter chats you participated in, edcamps you attended, and so on. Describe what you have accomplished as a result of these sessions and their limitations. This helps demonstrate that you will participate fully in the event and the impact it will have on your district's schools and teachers.

➤ Share helpful sessions. Provide a list of the available sessions that you plan to attend. Give a short description of each session and how you think it will benefit you and your school or district.

➤ Share your plans for after the event. Provide a plan for how you will share information with teachers. For example, you could host a mini-conference or edcamp, provide a series of trainings, create a train-the-trainer initiative with two or three teachers at each school, or make more informed decisions when purchasing products and programs.

➤ Be thrifty. Are you able to get a roommate? Use your own frequent flyer points? Making an effort to reduce costs helps encourage leadership to provide the remainder of the funds. Additionally, if you are in the process of writing a larger grant, you may be able to include this in your proposal. Many grants allow funding for educators to attend conferences with sessions that match the grant subject area.

Help Teachers Make Connections

As a coach it is easy to do things for the teachers, but is more impactful to show them how to find resources and assistance on their own. Previously, I worked for a professional development director who instructed our coaching staff that we should be "working ourselves out of a job." There will always be a need for coaches and new products and strategies for us to teach, but what teachers will find most valuable is if we can help them become self-reliant and confident in their abilities to use technology in their class-room—just as they are trying to help their students become empowered learners. The following ideas will help you inspire and empower teachers to make connections and begin exploring and researching technology tools and strategies on their own:

✦ Try an edcamp unconference. One of my favorite ways to help teachers make valuable connections is by hosting an edcamp or other type of uncon-ference. I am currently a co-founder and organizer for three edcamps in Florida that have brought educators together from more than thirty dis-tricts around our state. Edcamps energize and inspire teachers to try new ideas and provide connections they might not be able to make in their own district. For example, I have a friend who is the only game design teacher in her entire district. This can get lonely, but at an edcamp she may meet others in similar positions and begin a collaboration that is mutually beneficial. One benefit of hosting an edcamp rather than a traditional con-ference is that the Edcamp Foundation (**edcamp.org**) provides financial support, as well as guidance for creating your event. Another benefit of an edcamp is that the session topics are determined based on the participants' interests. This not only makes the event more exciting with the possibil-ities and potential, but it also ensures that the content will be timely and relevant to everyone who attends.

✦ Create a Twitter chat or hashtag for your school or district. The chats do not need to occur weekly or even monthly, but they will help teachers connect with others outside of their own team and school. You can also create a hashtag with monthly themes.

✦ Incorporate PLNs into your PD. You can easily incorporate PLN development during the professional development training that you offer. Allow participants to reflect on areas of need or where they are lacking in training or information, and provide time and resources for teachers to find groups, chats, blogs, and individuals to connect with online.

Create a Shared Vision

Collaborations and networking are often the first step toward a shared vision that leads to positive change. The ISTE Standards for Coaches encourage this with the Change Agent standard. Indicator 1a states that coaches should "create a shared vision and culture for using technology to learn and accelerate transformation through the coaching process," while 1e states that coaches should "connect leaders, educators, instructional support, domain experts and solution providers to maximize the potential of technology for learning" (ISTE Standards for Coaches, 1a and 1e, 2019).

This standard can only be accomplished with efforts to include all stakeholders in the strategic planning process. In my current district, we were fortunate to purchase a data analytics program that helps our department determine shared goals that can make the biggest impact. We then communicate these goals annually to school leaders, educators, parents, and students. Even with this process in place, however, there are always opportunities to improve.

For example, who in your school or district do you think feels on the outskirts of planning or often disregarded? I suspect positions these individuals fill would not vary much between our districts. These educators and support staff employees can provide us with insights that we would not receive otherwise, however, and could inform our school's goals. They meet regularly with individual or small groups of students, as well as parents, and have access to valuable information. To truly create a shared vision, all stakeholders need to feel part of the planning process. Even a short survey to ask for opinions and ideas can go a long way to make staff members feel supported and appreciated. Additionally, there is a tremendous amount of research, including that discussed in *The Wisdom of Crowds* by James Surowiecki, to show that the collective voice of many is more beneficial than the voice of a few experts.

Connect with Stakeholders

Reach out beyond your usual connections: Include instructional support staff in all communication with teachers. I have never had anyone complain about being included, but I have definitely received complaints when I neglected to include someone. Additionally, notify them of any educational technology training opportunities you are offering. In my Google Drive account, I have a folder with documents listing all staff members at my schools. When I communicate through email or other means, I review those documents to ensure that I do not miss anyone.

Communicate Your Shared Vision

The best way to ensure that your vision is understood and remembered is to share it in numerous ways and often. Here are some ideas for how to do this:

+ Train the trainer. The most effective method I have used to communicate a shared vision and goals is through a Train-the-Trainer initiative. In one district where I worked, we asked school administrators to select two teachers to be a part of our School Technology Leader program. Our first criterion was that these individuals were great teachers and well-liked amongst staff. We wanted teachers who could inspire others and who others would feel comfortable seeking out. Technology expertise was helpful but not as important as the other criteria. These technology leaders participated in yearlong training sessions, half face-to-face and half virtual, and they were required to present a certain number of sessions back in their schools.

- Offer consistent professional learning. I recommend creating a rubric to ensure that you are communicating a shared vision during all professional learning sessions. This should be shared with all edtech coaches and trainers, ensuring that you are meeting the needs of your teachers and delivering a consistent message. Often in schools, initiatives come and go, so teachers may tune out when we communicate a new philosophy or learning model. By providing a consistent message that teachers hear regularly in their training, teachers are more likely to see its relevance.

- Reach out through newsletters, websites, and other communications. Again, getting the message out in as many places as possible is key. The shared vision should definitely be included on your public and internal district website, along with any flyers distributed to parents and community stakeholders. Additionally, if you send a newsletter to teachers, this is a great way to communicate your progress toward goals and highlight teachers and schools who are finding unique and innovative ways to support your vision.

- Using these strategies consistently will communicate ideas to all stakeholders and help bring your vision to fruition.

 The best way to practice the strategies in this chapter is to get started with making connections. Using the hashtag #AuthenticEdVentures, share projects you have in the works, and let's work together to make them a success.

CHAPER 4

DESIGNING MEANINGFUL PROJECTS

With steadily increasing standards and expectations, along with interruptions such as active shooter drills, every minute counts in the classroom and every lesson needs to have the maximum impact in terms of student engagement and learning outcomes. Well-designed projects are not sufficient; we need to consciously assess how each project is benefiting our students and determine how we can maximize learning opportunities for all students throughout the day.

ISTE's Designer standard encourages teachers to "design authentic learning activities that align with content area standards and use digital tools and resources to maximize active, deep learning" (ISTE Standards for Educators, 5b, 2017). This chapter demonstrates ways to make projects meaningful by providing opportunities for students to create, evaluate, and synthesize information, as well as—most importantly—to provide an authentic purpose for the projects and presentations students complete in class. You can adapt most of these ideas for any grade level and multiple content areas.

Make Presentations Meaningful

When we as adults present reports and slideshows to our employers, they typically include an evaluation, some analysis, or a recommendation based on our research or findings. Similarly, classroom research should allow for the same types of evaluation and analysis, with opportunities for students to offer authentic solutions and ideas in their presentations. Now, with so much information at our fingertips, our focus can shift from content knowledge to making connections, digging deeper into history, and finding patterns between different historical events and time periods.

The need for this focus shift became particularly apparent to me when I was asked to judge a student website contest, for which students also presented research on their historical topic. After learning her project did not win, one student (respectfully) inquired as to why. This student presented a report that checked all the boxes, but it included little attempt at analysis, synthesis of information, or personal reflection. Throughout this student's academic career, she had learned that if you follow the rubric, you would score well. In this instance, the approach did not work—nor will it in the student's future. Few problems in adulthood come with a rubric. Similarly, problems we face as adults rarely have a clear solution. Thus, providing students with open-ended projects will help prepare them for the uncertainties they will face later in life.

As the way we access content evolves, our curriculum needs to evolve as well. There is still a need for students to memorize key information and calculate math quickly. However, a more balanced approach is needed, one that helps students practice future-ready, critical-thinking skills and deeper evaluation of concepts, such as tasking students with making comparisons between two products or asking students to synthesize information from multiple sources in order to present a cohesive argument. The sections that follow provide strategies and examples for helping students dig deeper when writing and completing projects. Students are capable of doing this; practice is the key to getting them there, and that takes time.

Establish the "Why"

Projects will undoubtedly take more time than you originally planned. Even as a teacher who embraced PBL and often ignored pacing and time-lines, having a project go too far beyond the time allotted caused me stress. I remember venting to my media specialist once about how long my elementary students were taking to create book trailers—there was so much more I needed to cover, so many standards to meet. She came to me the next day with a list of thirty or so standards that were incorporated in the book trailer lesson. After seeing this, I calmed down and embraced the process.

The moral here is to begin with your standards and incorporate standards from across several content areas into your projects if possible. This will help justify the amount of time the projects take. Cross-curricular projects can be more challenging in secondary classrooms, where students transition to different classrooms with specialized instructors for each content area. In these cases, it is helpful to build a cohesive team of educators willing to collaborate in these types of endeavors.

Beyond the Standards

Beyond the standards, try to imbue your project or presentation with a deeper purpose. One way to do this is through *tiered projects* (see Lesson Plans 4.3 and 4.4). To understand how these projects work, consider the last collaborative project you worked on for your career and how you delivered your part to group members and other audiences. How interested were they in your part? Was your information needed for coworkers to create their parts of the project or for a larger goal? Chances are your group members and audience were interested, and your contributions were used as part of a larger project. This tiered approach appears in most careers, as well. Think about a law office, in which attorneys and paralegals are working together to conduct research for a case that only one or two attorneys will deliver in court, or a construction project in which contractors, project managers, structural engineers, and architects all contribute their skills. This creates accountability for the group members, as well as a greater purpose for completing their work.

In most classrooms, however, group projects seldom rely on information from others or serve a larger purpose. Information is divided into sections, and students follow a rubric in order to achieve a good grade. As for the student who came up short in the website contest, this approach is not enough anymore. In contrast, our goal should be to create projects with individual accountability for students that serve a larger purpose or collective goal.

For example, when designing a class garden, a teacher instructs students to each research a flower or plant that they think should be included in a garden. Next, the entire class works to establish criteria for how students will select which plants should be included. Do they want native plants that require less upkeep? Plants that bloom throughout the year? Through this process, students learn that individual contributions and talents make the project successful. As students present their findings, their classmates (and teacher) are genuinely interested, listening to evaluate whether that particular plant or flower would be a good fit.

When I facilitated this lesson in a fourth-grade classroom recently, students became upset when their plant was not chosen for the garden project. One in particular threatened to rip up her report because her plant was not being used. This was a great opportunity to show students what authentic research is like. Sometimes we learn what *does not* work, rather than what *does*. This information can be just as valuable. I talked with that student, and the entire class, about what would happen if we chose a certain plant that was invasive or required more upkeep than we were able to manage. Students began to see that their research was valuable even if their plant was not selected for the garden, and that the collective information helped us achieve a successful product.

Another easy way to establish purpose during a project is to incorporate student interests. It is likely that their engagement and level of commitment to the project will increase when they are learning something they like and understand. Some suggested topics by grade levels are:

+ K–2: Animals, nature, play and toys, video games, sports

+ 3–5: Animals, children's rights and privileges, video games, sports

+ 6–8: Social justice, children's rights and privileges, video games, sports

+ 9–12: Social justice, social media, career-oriented topics, school safety, sports, fashion

You can conduct an interest survey, such as the one shown in Figure 4.1, with your class to determine student interests and hobbies. You can find a copy at **bit.ly/SurveyStudentInterests** and add choices as students indicate other topics of local interest that are not currently included.

Student Interest Survey

Form description

:::

If you could choose a magazine or non-fiction book to read, what would it be about? Check the *
boxes next to all the topics you enjoy.

☐ Animals

☐ Sports and athletes

☐ Cars

☐ Cooking and crafts

☐ Health and exercise

☐ Art, music or dance

☐ Science

☐ History

ESTABLISH AN AUTHENTIC PURPOSE

When I think back to my years in the classroom, I can remember times when I tried to engage students by doing something outlandish—wearing silly costumes, cooking food, and so on. This is a great way to capture their attention, but if the gimmick does not support a deeper level of learning, then it could actually be causing more harm than good. Sundar (2019) describes these distractions as "seductive details" in her article "Cut It Out: Learning with Seductive Details." Essentially, students pay more attention to the distraction, rather than the main topic, missing the main point of what they should be learning. This concept reminds me of times early in my teaching career. When my students would tell their parents, "We just played today," I would feel like an effective teacher, able to engage students in learning they recognized as play. Later, I realized that students need to be aware of their learning goals and understand what they know and what they need to learn. ISTE recognizes this as well with the Empowered

Learner standard, which states, "students leverage technology to take an active role in choosing, achieving and demonstrating competency in their learning goals, informed by the learning sciences" (ISTE Standards for Students, 2016).

So, how do you accomplish this goal and engage students without the gimmicks? One way is by encouraging risk-taking.

Encourage Risk-Taking

There are numerous ways to facilitate lessons that encourage students to take risks in their learning. This is something that occurs organically in science class with inquiry questions, labs, and trial-and-error activities. However, in math and writing, students quickly learn that there is a "right" way to do something, which is doing a disservice to our students. Consider the famous, much-loved Alice in Wonderland poem "Jabberwocky"—which is essentially a bunch of gibberish. When we expose students to only one way of writing, we deny them the opportunity to express this type of creativity.

Here are a couple examples of activities that will help you encourage risk-taking in your classroom:

+ Finding Bad Solutions. You can encourage risk-taking by engaging in brainstorming and asking questions such as, "What would be the worst solutions to this problem?" Later, ask students to consider how to make some of those solutions better. This is a form of divergent thinking, which is discussed in more detail in the "Get Started with Brainstorming" section.

+ "Yes, And" Exercises. While brainstorming for ideas or solutions, require students to accept all ideas, adding to them only with a "Yes, and . . ." phrase. This is a commonly used improvisation game, but it can make an impact in your classroom as well. Although it may not always result in working solutions, it can allow students to feel comfortable providing ideas.

- Risk-Taker Award. During problem-solving challenges and lessons, award the student or group who took the biggest risk. This can be a certificate or badge that recognizes their ability to take chances while learning.

- Epic Fail Wall. Consider creating a wall for epic fails in your classroom. You can include some famous ones, such as New Coke, Coca-Cola's back-fired attempt to change the taste of its flagship product in 1985. The most important thing to incorporate is the opportunity for students to reflect and demonstrate how they learned from their mistake. As with most ideas, you will need to gauge the maturity of your students. This idea may be more suited for secondary classrooms.

The best way to encourage risk-taking is to keep assignments and projects open-ended. When students understand there are multiple ways to solve a problem, they are more likely to try. I recommend Dan Meyer's TEDxNYED Talk, "Math Class Needs a Makeover" (**bit.ly/2PfVDAX**), which offers more insights about this.

Attention Getters and Activating Prior Knowledge

The beginning of your lesson is when you either win or lose your audience. Rather than rely on a gimmicky "seductive details," use an attention getter with substance. Make sure your attention getter is something that all students understand, not relying on too much background knowledge or prior learning prerequisites. For example, if your project discusses renewable and non-renewable resources, rather than showing a video with vocabulary and concepts students may not understand, instead show a video or photo of a trash dump and ask students to briefly write, draw, or discuss their reaction. Here are a few other ideas for attention getters to introduce a project:

- Perform an experiment. Bring out your inner Bill Nye and introduce an experiment or lab to get students thinking about the topic and project. This will inspire students to develop inquiry questions and encourage them to answer their questions as they learn throughout the unit.

+ Mute a video. Show a short video clip that demonstrates a topic or standard with minimal onscreen text. Mute the video, and ask students to work in small groups to watch the video, pause periodically, and write words that might be in the video clip. This gets students thinking about the topic—what they already know and what they think they may be learning during the lessons. Alternately, you could use this approach to inspire creative writing by asking students to write a script for a muted video.

+ Seek to inspire. If your topic is meant to initiate action, consider reading a story or poem to inspire passion in your students. For example, if your students will be researching ways to help save endangered animals, you could share the TEDxYouth@BeaconStreet Talk by John Linehan titled "Saving Animals, Saving the Future" (**bit.ly/33nH7Q5**).

+ Ask a driving question. Students (and most people, for that matter) love a realistic and achievable challenge. Even if they do not understand quite how to answer the driving question in the beginning, they will work harder and pay more attention as they learn more, helping them answer the question later. When creating driving questions, I am always reminded of Vygotsky's Zone of Proximal Development as well as really good games. Both demonstrate the importance of providing enough challenge to keep us interested but not so much that the task seems nearly impossible (Shabani, et al., 2010). The PBLWorks website (**pblworks.org**) includes resources to help you create engaging driving questions. One example is the *PBL Blog* post by John Larmer titled "A Tricky Part of PBL: Writing a Driving Question" (**bit.ly/2PfVTzV**; you will need to create a free account in order to view the post).

+ Display or show an example. Showing an example of a completed project can serve as inspiration and also provide students with a better understanding of your expectations. Finding a good example is easy once you have taught a lesson for a year or two, but if this is your first time initiating a project, it can be challenging. Often, I create my own example or enlist the help of other teachers' kids, or my own nephews

(Figure 4.2). One challenge with providing examples is the tendency for students to mimic the example. I remember many times in my classroom stating, "Hmm, so your story is about a refrigerator that comes to life as a superhero. This is almost exactly like my example." With perfect second-grade logic, the student would say, "No, your story had a *dishwasher* that came to life as a superhero." One remedy for this is to tell students that you expect their idea to be unique: "Think of an idea you feel confident is not like anyone else's idea." You can ask students to write their idea for your approval before they begin the project, as well. After a few rejections, they usually come up with an original idea. Try to phrase these rejections in the form of questions to help students realize the issue on their own.

4.2 My nephews Brady and Nate often serve as beta testers for my example projects.

GET STARTED WITH BRAINSTORMING

Now that you have your students' attention with your project introduction, it's time for them to begin brainstorming ideas for their own projects. The two basic types of brainstorming are convergent and divergent thinking. *Convergent thinking* is more linear and usually consists of narrowing down a topic with pros and cons, or similar methods. *Divergent thinking* is more abstract and can include concept maps to connect ideas, while encouraging participants to take risks and present lots of ideas, even if they may not seem feasible at the time.

My favorite brainstorming activity incorporates both convergent and divergent thinking:

1. To begin, ask students to generate lots of ideas, even those that are silly or seem impossible. Encourage them to take risks and write down everything that comes to mind, even if it seems impractical. To encourage this risk-taking, tell each group that their goal is to come up with 50 ideas (or another number depending on the grade level). Make the goal something that is just out of reach, given the time limit. Again, think of Vygotsky and how you can give a "just right" level of challenge.

2. Students consider the ideas and identify three to five that could possibly work, with some tweaking. Using divergent thinking, students then create a concept map, connecting and expanding on the ideas they have.

3. Students next move into convergent thinking, in which they start identifying pros and cons for their top two or three ideas, narrowing it down to one or two ideas the group agrees would work best.

4. Finally, students revise their idea and present it to their audience. This process might take an entire class period but is worth it to help students ideate creative ideas and effective solutions to problems.

After brainstorming, review student ideas before they begin creating their projects. This step will help deter far-fetched ideas, such as flying cars. When you find one of these, steer students toward more realistic options by asking questions like:

+ "Does this already exist?"

+ "How will you build a prototype?"

+ "Do you have enough scientific knowledge to create this?"

If there are certain standards you would like students to master during a project, it is vital that you redirect them when their ideas are off-topic or too unrealistic. This brainstorming activity can be adapted in an online learning classroom by asking students to brainstorm their ideas in an online document such as Microsoft Word or Google Docs. An online brainstorming template can be found at **bit.ly/3iD8M47**. Students could also brainstorm in a videoconference breakout room.

Transforming Take-Home Projects

Some of our smallest decisions can have long-reaching consequences: Paper or plastic? Eat here or to go? Take-home or in-class? Many teachers opt for take-home projects, as they minimize time, cost, and student-support barriers. I prefer in-class projects, especially when teaching for mastery, because I find that at-home projects do not typically support this model. When students complete projects in class, teachers are there to ask questions, provide scaffolding, and help students develop a deeper understanding of concepts. At home, we are unable to assist students or determine if they truly understand their work.

When I taught second grade, we initiated a Flea Market Day project, teaching students about spending and saving, supply and demand, and other economics concepts. This was a typical opportunity for a take-home project, as it would take up a lot of class time and required supplies not available in the classroom. Other teachers tasked students with developing their products and services at home. However, I opted to facilitate the project in class. The day of the market, other classes featured products and services obviously designed by parents—some even purchased complete Skee-ball games. I worried my students would be upset with their kid-designed products, but they were proud of the products they created on their own in class (Figure 4.3)—and they were very popular with market-goers. The students were better at determining what would sell than I and their well-intentioned parents were. After all, who better to know what kids like than other kids? When I stepped back and allowed students to problem solve and create, they exceeded my expectations.

4.3   Student-designed games for the Flea Market Day project, such as this Beyblade Tournament, enabled students to problem solve and create for a meaningful purpose.

Turn Take-Home Projects into Class Projects

Although take-home projects do have their purpose, as you'll see in the next section, simply to save classroom time and funds shouldn't be one of them. With a little innovation, you can adapt typical take-home projects to in-class projects while still ensuring productive class time and encouraging parent participation:

How do I fund needed supplies? Ask students to create a supply list and research the amount of money needed for supplies not found at home or in the classroom. Provide them with a budget, and ask students to write letters home explaining the project and asking for the supplies. With younger students, you can create a letter template with blanks to fill in, but older students should be able to write their own letters. Figure 4.4 is an example of my Flea Market Day project letter template. If you work with families who are unable to send in supplies, send your students' letters to your local education foundation or business to ask for donations. It is difficult for adults to refuse requests that come directly from kids.

4.4 Rather than send the project home, have students send a letter requesting project supplies.

Dear _____,

    Our class is studying Economics during Social Studies this month. We are excited to learn about Goods and Services, Trade, Saving and Spending, and Supply and Demand. Our final project for this unit will be a Flea Market. Our class will be creating and selling products and services for other classes to buy.

    My group will be selling _____

_____. Below I have listed some materials we will need to create our good/service. We would appreciate your help sending in some of these items.

_____

_____

_____

                          Thank you,

                          _____

- How do I find time in class? Providing students with time to complete every phase of a project in class can be difficult. I recommend allowing students to brainstorm, bring in supplies, and begin creating their project at school. Later, students can take their project home to complete. This way you ensure that the project is their original idea, while saving time in class. This may not be feasible with hands-on collaborative projects or those that require specialized equipment, but it will work in other instances.

- How can I make parents feel included? If parents feel left out of the project process, you can invite them to help the day of the event or presentations, or provide them with the project rubric so they can help their child assess their own progress. This allows parents to be involved, while at the same time ensuring students are given the opportunities and space to become Knowledge Constructors and Innovative Designers (ISTE Standards for Students, 2016).

- How do I facilitate "in-class" projects in a virtual classroom? Incorporating projects in a virtual classroom can be tricky—but not impossible. I recommend utilizing videoconference breakout rooms to provide time for students to brainstorm project ideas with their partners. They will have the added constraint of selecting materials that can be found inside their homes. Yes, they will technically be creating their project at home; however, the brainstorming and project creation steps will be completed with classmates online and with the guidance of a teacher.

When Take-Home Projects Work

Take-home projects *can* be beneficial in some instances. For example, getting your students to connect with their families and learn more about their culture, careers, and interests can have a positive impact for their families. When implementing take-home projects, be sure to consider equity. We are not always aware of the economic situations affecting our students, so it is best to provide supplies whenever possible. Additionally, some parents are working more than one job to provide for their families and will not have time to complete extensive projects with their children. Having this awareness can help you make decisions that meet the needs of all your students and families. Here are a few ideas that work well as take-home projects:

+ Cultural Subjects. When reading a novel about a certain holiday or culture, create a cultural take-home project. Students interview family members to learn about traditions and their family history. In Florida, our second graders learn about immigration. What a great way to connect families, by asking students when their family came to America and how they got there. Back in class, this leads to interesting discussions and learning opportunities.

+ Crowdsourced Ideas. Encourage students to crowdsource ideas with their families. For example, students in a health class could create a list of tips for healthy eating by interviewing family members to gather ideas and resources to share in class. Or students in an economics course could ask family members to help explore pros and cons for purchasing certain stocks. To avoid students just "getting the answers" from parents, create guidelines to ensure that students are engaging in discussions and asking questions to learn more about the ideas. Students will learn the benefit of collaboration and that learning is a lifelong adventure.

+ Surveys. Students combine math with other content topics and survey family members. In an Industrial Revolution lesson, for example, students could conduct research at school and then create survey questions to ask parents at home, such as "Which of these jobs would you have had during the Industrial Revolution?" The student then provides a list of possible answers for each question. After conducting their surveys and tallying the results, students share their findings back at school and compare their data. Along with adding math, this project encourages families to initiate discussions around school topics.

LESSON PLANS

The following lesson plans incorporate ways to encourage your students to find a deeper meaning in the projects you initiate. You will see evidence of student choice, effective brainstorming, and other concepts to help students become more engaged in what they are learning.

LESSON PLAN 4.1 Historical Thinking Project

Subject: Social Studies/ELA research

Target Grades: 4–12

Duration: 1–2 class periods

Used in Canadian classrooms, the Historical Thinking Project (**historicalthinking.ca**) is a social studies curriculum that focuses on helping students think like historians and includes such concepts as:

+ Establishing historical significance: How do we decide what and whose stories to tell?

+ Analyzing cause and consequence: What are the causes that are hidden from view?

+ Understanding ethical dimensions of history: What do historical injustices and sacrifices mean for us today?

+ Identifying continuity and change: Does change always mean progress?

+ Taking historical perspectives: How can we ever understand the past?

+ Using primary source evidence: How do we know what we know? (Centre for the Study of Historical Consciousness, 2020)

In this lesson, students will conduct research about a historical event and curate primary and secondary source documents. Students will select Historical Thinking Project concepts and apply them to the event they researched, then present their findings to the class or another authentic audience.

Objectives

Grades 4–8 students will be able to:

+ Conduct research about important historical events.

+ Share historical findings in a presentation.

+ Read and comprehend informational texts independently and proficiently.

+ Evaluate and synthesize information about historic events.

Grades 9–12 students will be able to:

+ Conduct relevant research about important historical events.

+ Share historical findings in a presentation.

+ Analyze primary and secondary sources to locate evidence about events and attitudes during periods of history.

+ Write to evaluate and synthesize information about historic events.

Preparation

Materials:

+ Historical Thinking Project Posters (**historicalthinking.ca/posters**)

+ Finding Primary Source Documents (**bit.ly/3d1dOo6**)

+ Historical Thinking Project Rubric (**bit.ly/2Z38KeG**)

+ Historical Thinking Project Choice Menu (**bit.ly/3egAvVO**)

Advanced Preparation:

✦ Display Historical Thinking Project Posters in the classroom or distribute to students digitally.

✦ Preview links listed in Finding Primary Source Documents to ensure there are sufficient documents to align with the topic you chose.

Standards Implemented in Lesson 4.1

ISTE STANDARDS FOR EDUCATORS	ISTE STANDARDS FOR STUDENTS	CONTENT AREA STANDARDS
Citizen 3b, 3c Designer 5b Facilitator 6a	Digital Citizen 2b, 2c Knowledge Constructor 3a, 3b, 3c, 3d Creative Communicator 6a, 6d Global Collaborator 7b, 7c	Students will use ELA research standards and informational reading skills while engaging in social studies and history concepts.

Instructions

Ask students to define *historian* and list features of a historian's job. Explain that students have the opportunity to become historians and analyze historical documents. Review the definition of *primary sources.* Divide students into groups or allow them to work individually. Provide students with the Historical Thinking Project Rubric, Finding Primary Source Documents, and Historical Thinking Project Choice Menu documents.

Provide time for students to conduct research, deciding which Historical Thinking Project concepts to include in their presentations. Students continue conducting research and curating primary and secondary sources.

Students meet to begin creating their presentations, dividing up roles and/or slides. Periodically stop and show student work, identifying misconceptions and addressing things students are doing well, as well as areas needing improvement.

 Provide students time to create their presentations and share them in your LMS or on a website such as Padlet. After students post their presentations, have them engage in peer review.

 Students submit their presentation in the class discussion and answer the questions: "How is your research and analysis similar to your classmates' research? How is it different? Why do you think that is?" Ask students to respond to at least two other classmates' presentations.

Extensions

Consider videoconferencing with a professional historian throughout this process. This person can provide tips prior to students beginning the research process and can review student work to make suggestions and point out areas of need.

Here are a few other ideas for implementing the Historical Thinking Project in your classroom:

✦ When reading a historical fiction novel with your students, consider reading other poems or short stories that offer a different perspective about events that are taking place. Book studies are also a great way to uncover the causes and consequences of historical events featured in the novel.

✦ When studying Black history, ask students to analyze primary source documents and learn how people were treated and segregated prior to the Civil Rights Movement. Another option is to introduce the ethical dimensions concept and evaluate how actions taking place years ago affect us today.

✦ Ask students to investigate a period of history and consider why certain people's stories were told and not others. Students research "hidden figures" who made a contribution but are not widely recognized, finding a creative way to tell their story.

ONLINE AND REMOTE LEARNING ADAPTATION

Introduce the project during a videoconference session. Students use shared online documents to curate primary and secondary sources and to organize their presentations. Later, students add their presentations in an LMS or using a tool such as Padlet.

LESSON PLAN 4.2 The Feynman Project

Subject: Science, ELA research

Target Grades: 6–12

Duration: 2–3 weeks

Nobel Award–winning physicist Richard Feynman believed that a scientist does not truly understand a concept unless they can explain it in simple words to a kindergarten student. Encouraging students to dig deeper in their understanding of topics, the Feynman Technique, therefore, states:

1. Choose a concept.

2. Teach it to a kindergartner (or young student).

3. Identify gaps or errors in your understanding and continue to study and research.

4. Simplify and revise.

Standards Implemented in Lesson 4.2

ISTE STANDARDS FOR EDUCATORS	ISTE STANDARDS FOR STUDENTS	CONTENT AREA STANDARDS
Citizen 3c Designer 5b Facilitator 6a Digital Citizen 2b, 2c Knowledge Constructor 3a	Creative Communicator 6a, 6d Global Collaborator 7c	Students will engage in science standards, along with ELA research, informational reading, and presentation skills.

I learned about this method when I collaborated on a project with Andrew Hutcheson, an AP Physics teacher in my district; his students presented a physics topic to students at our local elementary schools (Figure 4.5). We provided the high-school students with a rubric, elementary standards, and Mayer's Principles of Multimedia Learning (see Chapter 2). Then students worked in groups, selected a topic, and decided how they would present their information to the elementary students. Products ranged from traditional Microsoft PowerPoint presentations, to live demonstrations of leaf blower hovercrafts, with some videos, online games, and ebooks thrown in as well. Students deepened their content knowledge, working through theories, laws, and concepts in unfamiliar ways.

4.5 High-school students practiced the Feynman Technique to teach physics concepts to elementary students.

In this lesson plan, older students will use the Feynman Technique to create presentations they will then teach to younger students. The best part about using the Feynman Technique is that it encourages students to adopt the iterative process that is essential for scientists and many other careers.

Objectives

Grades 6–12 students will be able to:

+ Simplify science concepts and explain them.

+ Create a science lesson and present it in a clear, concise, and interesting manner.

Preparation

Materials:

+ Feynman Project Rubric (**bit.ly/3cZzeCf**)

+ Feynman Project Resources (**bit.ly/36s3seA**)

Advanced Preparation:

+ Contact elementary schools and teachers to begin arranging class visit dates and expectations.

+ Contact your school administration for field trip/off-campus permission forms for your students.

Instructions

Explain the Feynman Technique to students. Ask them to test it out with some concepts you are currently studying in class. Discuss how well they were able to simplify the content. Ask for volunteers who have younger siblings: Would their siblings be able to understand the concept?

If not, then ask what they could do to help their siblings understand. Provide students with the Feynman Project Rubric and lists of standards for kindergarten through fourth grade. Divide them into groups and encourage them to review the standards and select one.

Students engage in divergent and convergent thinking to brainstorm ideas for their lessons. Begin by setting a timer for 3–5 minutes. Ask students to list all the ideas they can think of for their lesson (divergent thinking). Remind them not to critique or veto ideas. Ask students to consider their options and narrow them down to two or three solid ideas (convergent thinking). They will make pros-and-cons charts, debating the merits of each idea until they are able to narrow it down to their top one or two choices. These ideas should include how they will deliver the content (video, presentation, ebook, etc.), along with their lesson idea (Bill Nye–style experiment, dress up like aliens, etc.).

Students watch videos and read articles to learn more about Mayer's Principles of Multimedia Learning and/or copyright guidelines. Students review physics concepts that align with the elementary standards.

Provide time for students to work on their lesson both in and out of class. Ask students to provide you with a list of supplies they need to execute their project. Students find one or two children to beta test their lesson. Students reflect on how their "dress rehearsal" went and then make changes as needed. Students may also post their projects in an LMS discussion or similar online platform to gather peer feedback.

Students present their lessons to nearby elementary schools or online.

Extensions

If it is not possible for students to visit elementary schools, they can share their lessons virtually. Some of these lessons might be added to district curriculum maps, increasing opportunities for an authentic audience.

ONLINE AND REMOTE LEARNING ADAPTATION

Begin by describing the project in a live videoconference session. Provide students with the elementary grade level standards (either as an online document or links to them), so they can begin selecting or creating a project and/or presentation. Students use videoconferencing and shared online documents to conduct additional research and exchange ideas with their teammates. Next, provide links to the Mayer's Principles of Multimedia Learning and copyright information in an online document. When completed, students share their projects in their LMS or another online platform and gather peer reviews. Students post their projects online so elementary schools can access them and provide feedback.

LESSON PLAN 4.3 Garden Tiered Project

Subject: Science

Target Grades: K–8

Duration: 2–3 weeks

With tiered projects, students complete tasks or mini-projects that will later connect to a larger class project or initiative. In this example, the class is creating a garden space for their school. Students will conduct research about plants and flowers and then share this information with their peers. This research will help determine which types of seeds should be planted, along with care and management of the plants chosen. After the initial research, students establish criteria for their selection and learn that although their plant may not have been chosen, they contributed helpful information that led to a better class garden.

Standards Implemented in Lesson 4.3

ISTE STANDARDS FOR EDUCATORS	ISTE STANDARDS FOR STUDENTS	CONTENT AREA STANDARDS
Citizen 3c Designer 5b Facilitator 6a	Digital Citizen 2b, 2c Knowledge Constructor 3a, 3b Global Collaborator 7b, 7c	Students will engage in ELA research and informational reading standards while they learn about plants and habitats in science.

Objectives

Grades K–8 students will be able to:

✦ Conduct research to learn more about plants and plant care.

✦ Create presentations to effectively share their findings.

✦ Develop criteria for selecting items.

✦ Work cooperatively and contribute to a class project.

Preparation

Materials:

✦ Garden tools

✦ Soil, landscaping products

✦ Seeds (after students make their selections)

✦ Planting a Garden Checklist (**bit.ly/2XopJpv**)

Advanced Preparation:

✦ Secure a location for your garden.

✦ Confirm permission to plant your garden.

Instructions

Show pictures of some gardens. Ask students what they think it takes to plan and care for a garden. List student responses and discuss. Explain that students will help you design and create a class garden. They will research plants and flowers that could be placed in the garden. Their research will be used to select the plants, as well as learn how to care for the garden.

Students work in groups of two or three to begin researching plants. They select one plant they feel will be a good option and another that they feel should not be included in the garden. This is a good time to talk about evidence. If students feel a plant should or should not be included, they will need to explain and provide reasons. Later, they will need to demonstrate how their plan does or does not meet the criteria the class agrees upon.

  Students will organize and curate their research and then present it to the class. This can be done in face-to-face Speed Dating presentations (see Chapter 2) while other students take notes or can be placed online.

Students will organize and curate their research and then present it to the class. This can be done in face-to-face Speed Dating presentations (see Chapter 2) while other students take notes or can be placed online.

After students present their findings, bring the students together to develop criteria for selecting the plants. On a chart paper or digital display, write, "What should we consider when choosing plants for our garden?" You can get things started by asking questions such as, "Do we want plants that are easy to maintain? Colorful plants? Plants that grow well in lots of sunlight?" During this time, visit the garden location to help select criteria to best meet the needs of this space. Students begin nominating plants that fit the criteria. Students discuss each plant nominated and later vote to determine which plants to include.

  Students create supply lists in a shared online document and write a letter to parents or local garden centers to request supplies. While some students work on creating the garden, others will establish a maintenance plan. Students continue to maintain their garden throughout the year, and revisit their criteria at the end of the year to determine any changes to make.

Extensions

Students design their garden using a landscape design app such as iScape (**iscapeit.com**), which offers a free thirty-day trial. Students can also invite a landscape architect to visit their classroom (either live or virtually) to share tips for design and plant maintenance.

> ### ONLINE AND REMOTE LEARNING ADAPTATION
>
> Students conduct research and present their ideas to their classmates using a videoconferencing tool or an online discussion forum. A virtual garden can be created using an app such as iScape, if students are unable to plant a live garden.

LESSON PLAN 4.4 Carnival Math Tiered Project

Subject: Math/Science

Target Grades: 6–8

Duration: 2–3 weeks

With tiered projects, students complete tasks or mini-projects that will later connect to a larger class project or initiative. In this example, students are tasked with creating a carnival game they can ensure will make money during a school fundraiser. Students will use math and physics concepts to help create a game that people feel they can win, although it is unlikely they will. Later students will select the games that have the best chance of making the most money and operate them at their school carnival or fundraising event.

Standards Implemented in Lesson 4.4

ISTE STANDARDS FOR EDUCATORS	ISTE STANDARDS FOR STUDENTS	CONTENT AREA STANDARDS
Citizen 3b Designer 5a, 5b Facilitator 6a, 6b, 6c	Digital Citizen 2b, 2c Knowledge Constructor 3a, 3d Innovative Designer 4a, 4b, 4c, 4d Creative Communicator 6a, 6c, 6d Global Collaborator 7c	Students will use speed, probability, data analysis, and math computation during this project. Students will engage in science force and motion standards.

Objectives

Grades 6–8 students will be able to:

✦ Apply math and science concepts to design a product.

✦ Use probability to determine the likelihood of an event occurring.

✦ Use computation skills to determine the amount of money their game can make depending on how many people play it.

✦ Design a product that will appeal to their intended audience.

Preparation

Materials:

✦ Various supplies to create carnival games

✦ Carnival Math Rubric (**bit.ly/3gtK8Bp**)

✦ "Carnival Scam Science—and How to Win" video (**bit.ly/2BIVTp1**)

✦ Optional: 3D printer to create game parts

Advanced Preparation:

✦ If possible, secure funding to purchase supplies requested by students to create their projects. In the past, I have written open-ended grants for these types of projects and encouraged students to submit requests for the supplies they need.

Instructions

 Show Mark Rober's video "Carnival Scam Science—and How to Win" to students and then discuss the math and science skills used to create these games. Discuss the three types of carnival games described in the video: chance games, skill games, and scam games. Discuss examples of each type of game and talk about how carnival games continue to trick people and have not changed much for many years.

  Group students and provide them time to brainstorm ideas and conduct research to begin creating their carnival game. Provide students with a budget and ask them to submit a request for supplies. Inform students that their design needs to convince people that they *can* win the game, even though it is unlikely. Students will need to poll people to determine whether they feel they can win the game.

 Students review any math or science concepts needed to complete this project. Students will continue their research and begin creating a draft for their project in a shared online document.

 Order supplies, and provide students with time to design a marketing plan for their games. When the supplies arrive, provide time for students to build and test their games. Students will need to determine the probability that a person will win the game by testing the game with a variety of people. They will need to explain how they used math and physics concepts to help create their game.

 Students select a prize for their game and will present a report detailing how much money their game will make for the fundraiser, depending on how many people play their game. For example, their report may say, "If 50 people play our game, we will make *[calculated number]* dollars for the fundraiser. If 100 people play our game, we will make *[calculated number]* dollars for the fundraiser." Students should deduct the amount for purchasing game supplies, as well as the amount for prizes to determine total anticipated earnings for their game.

Students share their presentation and game with class-mates, asking questions and providing feedback. Students select the carnival games to include in their fundraiser or school event.

Extensions

Students create videos in a similar style to Mark Rober, explaining their games and how they work. In the video, they must include the math and science concepts they used to make people feel like they can win the game.

> ### ONLINE AND REMOTE LEARNING ADAPTATION
>
> Students conduct research and collect data while working online. They may not be able to create and test their prototypes, unless each student has the necessary supplies in their homes. One alternative is to write grants for the supplies and ship them to students' houses, but this will require extra work for the teacher. Another option is to task students with creating their game from household recycled materials.

Coach's Connection

The ISTE Learning Designer standard calls on coaches to "collaborate with educators to develop authentic, active learning experiences that foster student agency, deepen content mastery and allow students to demonstrate their competence" (ISTE Standards for Coaches, 4a, 2019). This begins with best practices in lesson planning and reflecting on how technology can enhance lessons and projects. This Coach's Connection assists coaches with helping teachers create lessons and projects with an intentional design and authentic purpose. Additionally, this section provides ways to recognize teachers who are already digging deeper with projects.

As coaches, our knowledge of instructional pedagogy is more important than our technological skills and expertise. In many instances, effective technology integration requires a large shift in pedagogy on the part of the teacher. It is the coach's role to help make this process as seamless as possible. We are tasked with training teachers to use devices with their students and to understand why certain instructional models produce greater learning outcomes, as well as how to initiate these strategies successfully.

Fortunately, there are methods and models available to help successfully navigate this process. With each of these tools and models, it is important to plan alongside your teachers and provide scaffolding as needed.

Demonstrate Backwards Design

Many educators are asked to use backwards design when planning; however, this process is often reserved for planning with curriculum teams or during professional learning events. It is easy to identify the benefits, but having the time for this level of planning can be a challenge. Integrating backwards design into planning sessions during your coaching helps teachers understand the benefits of using this model when planning lessons and projects with authentic purpose.

Here is how the process works in my coaching sessions:

1. Using backwards design, ask educators to identify the desired outcome (knowledge and skills) students should master. Consider Bloom's Taxonomy or Webb's Depth of Knowledge to determine what the progression of knowledge would be for that particular concept (Ormrod and Jones, 2018). For example, if a class is beginning a unit on the human body, you would want students to be able to:

   + Level 1: Identify vocabulary words such as organ, system, and heart rate.

   + Level 2: Learn how to measure a heart rate and classify organs into systems.

   + Level 3: Draw conclusions about why certain organs are important to stay healthy and what can happen if our organs are mistreated or damaged.

   + Level 4: Describe how our organs work together and explain the consequences if we neglect our bodies.

2. Coach teachers through this process but provide some leeway. Remember, the desired goal is for students to master the required concepts and to be able to apply this knowledge at a deeper level. You might feel a component belongs in level 3, while the teacher felt it was level 4. This is not important to point out to the teacher, especially if they are just starting to use backwards design for planning. There are a variety of interpretations, so my goal as a coach is to get teachers more comfortable with this process, while seeing the benefits. If they (or you) become bogged down or frustrated by the details, the process may not work.

3. Keep a separate list of classroom activities if they arise. As you list the concepts at each level, sometimes a teacher may list one or more activities, such as a PSA to teach others about the importance of taking care

of their bodies. When this occurs, add another list on your chart or document for activity ideas. Without blatantly correcting the teacher, they will begin to see the difference between concepts and activities. Throughout this coaching process, I recommend asking questions rather than correcting, similar to how you would with students in a classroom.

4. Work with teachers to determine the evidence students will provide to demonstrate mastery. This helps when planning assessments and determining how technology can be included. Help teachers consider various types of assessments, rather than traditional tests. If this is out of a teacher's comfort zone, ask them to consider adding one or two performance tasks to their traditional test.

5. Begin planning learning experiences and lessons that meet your criteria and that prepare students for the assessments you planned. This is a great time to incorporate an instructional model such as TPACK (see the "TPACK and Technology" sidebar). You can also incorporate the ISTE Standards for Students here to help the teacher determine if they are providing authentic learning experiences for their students.

Help Teachers Plan Authentic Assessments

One of the most frequent questions I hear when teachers begin implementing projects is, "How will I assess them?" The Learning Designer standard urges coaches to "help educators use digital tools to create effective assessments that provide timely feedback and support personalized learning" (ISTE Standards for Coaches, 4b, 2019). As we provide teachers with strategies for authentic assessments, technology has the opportunity to shine, because without it providing timely feedback and personalized learning would be difficult.

TPACK AND TECHNOLOGY

TPACK stands for technology, pedagogy, and content knowledge. Similar to the backwards design approach, educators first consider their content knowledge, basically *what* they need to teach. Next, they consider which strategies best work to help students master those standards, essentially *how* they will teach these skills or the pedagogy. Finally, after determining the research-based strategies that best align with these standards or skills, teachers consider *which* technology tools to include during these lessons.

TPACK works well to help educators consider when technology is useful. Sometimes technology is not the answer, and this model will clearly demonstrate that. One of my favorite questions to teachers is, "How is this technology or tool enhancing the lesson?" Most of the time, they can respond quickly and enthusiastically with keywords such as student engagement, efficiency, collaboration, and so on. But there are other times when the technology is little more than a digital worksheet and can even be detrimental. As coaches we are aware of this, but having a tool to help teachers come to this realization on their own is really beneficial.

One game coaches can facilitate during professional development training is the TPACK game (Figure 4.6). Whether you play with pieces of paper in cups or Dr. Matthew J. Koehler's digital version (**matt-koehler.com/the-tpack-game**), the rules are the same: Given random elements in two of the categories, such as geometry content (C) and museum-based learning (P), teachers brainstorm how to incorporate an element from the missing third category, which is technology (T) in this case. Ask teachers to play with T missing, as technology should be the last step in the backwards design model. This is meant to spark conversations and idea sharing, so if while playing online, they are provided a C and a P that do not align, let them click again for new options. They may receive options that are not relevant to their practice, and again I let them click again. It is interesting to hear the conversations and friendly debates that take place, and I am unable to recall a session in which at least one group did not decide to throw out the technology altogether.

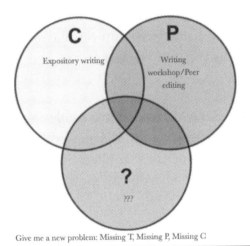

The TPACK Game – T

Given a random content area to teach, and pedagogical approach, figure out a technology and an activity to combine them

C — Expository writing

P — Writing workshop/Peer editing

? — ???

Give me a new problem: Missing T, Missing P, Missing C

4.6 In this round of the TPACK Game, educators are tasked with determining technology to use in a peer-editing workshop for expository writing.

Timely Feedback and Personalized Assessments

Most authentic assessments require teachers to manually grade assignments, so how do we as coaches help educators incorporate digital tools? There is a workaround: As students work through a project, there will be instances where a need for training arises. For example, while a student is writing a letter to a corporation to ask a question about their project, a teacher might notice some grammatical errors. Initially, the teacher may need to prepare or locate a tutorial video the student can watch and learn the necessary grammatical skill. Eventually, the teacher will collect a database of tutorials and short assessments for students to watch as needed. These short assessments are timely and relevant, providing individualized student support right when they need it, as well as instant feedback. An alternative to this is to ask students to help create tutorial videos and quizzes. Here are some tech tools that you can suggest to teachers for these short mini-lessons and assessments:

+ Nearpod. With Nearpod (**nearpod.com**), teachers are able to assign presentations that include videos, quizzes, polls, discussion boards, games, and other features to students for them to view and complete. Nearpod has a large gallery of lessons that you can assign to your students. Although a basic Nearpod subscription is free, various levels of paid subscriptions offer more features.

+ Khan Academy. Originally known for its instructional videos on diverse topics, Khan Academy (**khanacademy.org**) now includes quizzes and other content to accompany their videos. This is a great solution for personalized assessments during projects.

+ Google Forms. Enabling you to personalize content and deliver timely feedback, Google Forms (**forms.google.com**) allows you to insert videos and turn your form into a quiz. You can add sections, directing students to specific elements of the form depending on their responses to questions.

Authentic Assessments

Authentic assessments help teachers assess a deeper level of learning. They can range from student-created videos, infographics, songs, writing, live presentations, and many other mediums. When assisting teachers with developing and managing authentic assessments, ask yourself:

+ How can I assist teachers with fairly assessing students and providing clear expectations?

+ How can I assist teachers with collecting and grading authentic assessments in an efficient manner?

+ How can student choice and voice be included in the authentic assessment?

+ How can I assist the teacher with incorporating culturally responsive components in the assessment?

+ How can peer review or student feedback be incorporated in the authentic assessment?

You may have other questions you would like to include as well. The answers to these questions will depend on the grade level, teacher technology level, lesson content, student ability level, and other factors. Unfortunately, as coaches we will not always have time to work one-on-one with teachers to help with planning and creating assessments. Instead, consider grade-level sessions and incorporate this topic into your school and district-wide training.

Recognize Teachers Who Dig Deeper with Projects

Encourage teachers to reflect on their own lesson planning and level of rigor by recognizing those who are already doing so. By highlighting educators doing exemplary work with projects, you can inspire other teachers, as well as provide a model they can envision. Often, teachers do not have a clear picture of how an authentic project is different from what they are already doing. Conversely, other teachers may be implementing these outstanding models and strategies without realizing they are innovators and benchmark setters.

The Change Agent standard encourages coaches to "recognize educators across the organization who use technology effectively to enable high-impact teaching and learning" (ISTE Standards for Coaches, 1d, 2019). *Change agent* is a fitting title, as a large part of our role is prompting significant changes in classrooms and schools. From those on the outside, it might appear that coaches merely train teachers how to use technology tools. But we know better! In actuality, we are helping teachers transform their classroom by adding small group instruction, increasing collaboration, adding authenticity to learning, providing flexible learning environments, and more. By recognizing teachers, we are showcasing our skills as a coach. Think of it as a commercial for the services you offer. In fact, when providing these shout-outs to teachers doing amazing things, consider including a link, email address, or form for teachers to register for coaching sessions.

Here are some ways to recognize teachers who are implementing the ISTE standards or using innovative and effective strategies with their students:

+ Teacher Recognition Column. If you already send out a monthly or quarterly newsletter, add a section or column to recognize innovative teachers. When I started doing this, I never realized the impact it would have. I started out selecting teachers organically, just seeing innovative things I wanted to recognize. I asked other coaches to identify teachers as well. Before we knew it, school administrators were emailing us and suggesting teachers at their school. We realized how much schools and teachers like to be showcased, resulting in teachers working harder to create and implement innovative ideas and lessons.

+ Email Shout-Outs. If you do not have time for a monthly or seasonal newsletter, then consider recognizing teachers via email shout-outs to the schools you coach. Add pictures or short video clips to highlight their effective integration of technology.

- Survey and Share. During the COVID-19 pandemic, I began using Google Forms to survey teachers regarding the innovative ways they were using Zoom with their students. I compiled their suggestions into an infographic I shared, while also providing webinars to demonstrate the ideas and providing credit to those who found or innovated the activities. By reaching out to teachers, I was able to crowdsource ideas and showcase teachers. In the form, I also asked for suggestions on how teachers could provide fun and innovative "end of the year" virtual activities. This idea came about during a crisis, but it could align with a variety of events or lessons. I recommend keeping your form fairly specific because people have difficulty thinking of ideas when criteria and constraints are not provided.

- Staff Meeting Showcase. Ask school administrators for five minutes to recognize a teacher at their staff meeting. I recently showcased a fourth-grade teacher whose students documented their labs with the Clips app. After this short shout-out, I received numerous emails from teachers who were interested in learning more. At times I visit schools without seeing a single school administrator, so this presentation serves as a good reminder about the things I am doing as a coach to help support their teachers.

- Live Video Model Lessons. I have yet to implement this pie-in-the-sky idea, but I'm sharing it in the hope that you will. Begin by creating a private Facebook group that teachers in your district can join. I do not recommend allowing students, parents, or any other outside stakeholders; keep it a private place to learn where teachers feel they can be honest. From there, enlist the help of teachers willing to film live model lessons and showcase their lessons in the group. The sessions can be recorded for members unable to join live, and during the live broadcast teachers can ask questions that you save for the model teacher to answer. You can also jump in and monitor the class for a few minutes, allowing the teacher to answer any questions you are unable to answer yourself. The live video offers teachers a chance to see what is really happening in another classroom and how teachers handle "real-life" events that occur. Often, model videos are edited to eliminate any of those challenges. Also, live videos are fun; you never know what will happen, which is another reason to keep the group private. As with a Twitter chat, select specific days when you plan to broadcast live. Enlist the help of other coaches to record lessons to ensure sessions are available during all planning times. If you are the only edtech coach in your school or district, ask instructional coaches or media specialists to assist. Start small with this, piloting the idea with a few grade levels at one school, before expanding to include an entire district.

 Remember, making projects and presentations meaningful makes learning fun and engaging for students and teachers. I look forward to hearing how you adapted these lessons and coaches tips or created new ideas. Use the hashtag #AuthenticEdVentures on Twitter to let me know.

CHAPTER 5

PLANNING FOR THE UNEXPECTED

Classroom research and projects do not need to be a month-long process. You can create small and spontaneous opportunities for students to learn and explore their own interests and other topics. It always pains me to hear teachers say they will not have time to cover an important current event and build on the passion it could inspire in students. For example, 2019's historic all-female spacewalk was a great opportunity to explore women in STEM fields and encourage girls to embrace science and math concepts. To seize teachable moments like this, all you need is a bit of advanced planning—even if you're not sure what you're planning for. This chapter provides the organizational tools and strategies to help you, and demonstrates how writing, research, expository reading, scientific process, and other standards can be incorporated into the lessons. Great things happen when we take the detours; you just need to have your GPS handy!

Preparing for Teachable Moments

Teachable moments are often the most memorable lessons for both students and teachers. When students discover a new bug on the playground or a new student from another country arrives in the classroom, this prompts discussion and curiosity. This is true even for high-school students, when provided these same opportunities. Teachable moments allow students to practice the Empowered Learner standard, which states that "students understand the fundamental concepts of technology operations, demonstrate the ability to choose, use and troubleshoot current technologies and are able to transfer their knowledge to explore emerging technologies" (ISTE Standards for Students, 1d, 2016). With a little guidance, students can use technology to magnify objects, research unknown concepts and terms, scan a leaf to identify a tree, and many other uses. As students become comfortable with devices, apps, and programs, they are able to apply knowledge in novel situations, helping you seize the teachable moment.

STUDENT-FRIENDLY NEWS SOURCES

Current events and student interest–driven research provide opportunities to incorporate ELA nonfiction standards and concepts such as text features, reading for key details, and comparing and contrasting more than one text. With so many sources online, how do students target their searches? Our goal as educators is to help students locate sources that are valid, unbiased, and grade-level appropriate. The following news sources are a good starting point. All allow students to read or watch content, while some provide multiple, leveled reading passages for the same news story.

➤ Newsela. Also available in subscription versions, Newsela (**newsela.com**) allows students full access to current event articles for free. Newsela also personalizes articles for a variety of lexiles, ranging from grades 2–12. For elementary students, I download specific articles to print or share in our LMS, as there is some content that is not appropriate for this age group.

➤ TweenTribune. The Smithsonian TweenTribune (**tweentribune.com**) features free, leveled articles for students in grades K–12. Teachers can assign selected articles to students, along with quizzes and lesson plans.

➤ DOGOnews. DOGOnews (**dogonews.com**) contains current events news articles for kids. One nice feature is the ability to search by grade for interest levels, making it easier for you to find engaging content to meet the needs of your students.

➤ Youngzine. Youngzine (**youngzine.org**) brands itself as a wholesome and unbiased news source for young students. Similar to the other websites, Youngzine contains current events articles curated especially for kids.

Other news sources offer paid news content. For example, Discovery Education Streaming (**discoveryeducation.com/learn/partners**) includes video news segments through their Reuter's News partnership. Look for this if you already have a streaming membership or adopted their social studies textbook. Another news source for students in grades 1–5 is the News-O-Matic app (**newsomatic.org**). It is available for schools on iOS and Android devices and includes many interactive features. In its New & Trending section, BrainPOP (**brainpop.com/trending**) offers cartoon news videos for K–12 students.

Spontaneous Research Planning Documents

Along with time, lack of planning is a main reason teachers are unable to embrace teachable moments. It is difficult and scary to plan for the unknown, and sometimes it can seem like a waste of time to prepare for something that might never happen. When it comes to spontaneous and current events, however, a little planning can help you feel prepared to take on these teachable moments and curate resources ready to demonstrate the educational value of these projects.

These do not need to be lengthy projects with several revisions. If you provide opportunities for students to conduct short and relevant research, they will be less reluctant to dive into in-depth projects later. Stop and think a moment about the number of standards and skills needed to conduct research, and you can understand why students become overwhelmed during the process. Breaking these skills and standards into smaller parts implemented throughout the year will help students feel more comfortable and confident in their research abilities.

One of the best ways to prepare is to find and create planning documents in advance. These should include:

+ A general lesson plan including any relevant ELA reading and writing standards, with space to add other content standards.

+ A presentation, infographic, or document that will help students perform safe and effective searches, as well as locate valid sources. The C.A.R.S. (credibility, accuracy, reasonableness, and support) checklist is a good reference for this; Andy Spinks offers a downloadable version at **andyspinks.com/evaluating-websites**. Another useful resource is Kathy Schrock's Guide to Evaluating Websites (**schrockguide.net**).

+ Planning forms for students to complete as they begin their research. Visit **bit.ly/2WWkpea** for a template you can copy and adapt to fit your needs.

- A website or documents with links to kid-friendly research websites such as DKfindout! (**dkfindout.com**), National Geographic Kids (**kids.nationalgeographic.com**), and school or district databases. For secondary classrooms, contact your media specialist to determine which databases they offer, and include these links on your resource page. Secondary students can begin to search using scholarly journals such as Google Scholar (**scholar.google.com**), although they will need support and scaffolding for this.

- A menu of ways for students to present their findings. Options can include a traditional presentation, video, poster or infographic, ebook, or song they compose. Check out **bit.ly/2PuZfiR** for a sample research project menu.

Student-Designed Service Projects

Throughout the year, usually when you least expect it, events may arise that encourage fundraisers and other service-oriented projects in schools. Whether to aid hurricane victims on the other side of the country or a local family displaced by a fire, Table 5.1 suggests a few ways you can integrate service and fundraising projects into your curriculum.

Service projects are challenging to implement with secondary-school schedules. However, these students are more self-sufficient and able to perform tasks with a little support from teachers. One way to support student-created initiatives is to add service hours to student volunteer logs, as well as share their project with other school employees. Depending on the class and content topics, there may be relevant connections, allowing other teachers to provide some time in class for students to work on these projects. There is also an Applied Google Skills video course for high-school students to help them plan and manage a community service project. Visit **applieddigitalskills.withgoogle.com** to learn more.

TABLE 5.1 Teaching with Service Projects

WRITING	MATH
• During ELA station rotations, have students write donation request letters to be mailed or posted on social media. • Students write articles for the school newspaper or class newsletter to showcase their project and ask for help.	• Students keep a tally of the money donated (although the teacher should hold the actual money). • In upper grades, students create and manage spreadsheets to keep track of the various types of funding and money raised.
SOCIAL STUDIES	**STEM/STEAM**
• Students can learn about being good citizens by raising money, creating items for houseless people, and bringing in supplies for nursing homes. After participating, students can reflect on what it means to be a good citizen and how it felt to help others.	• In technology or art class, students can design an app or website to showcase their service learning project. • In a STEM elective, students can brainstorm ideas and create, test, and redesign their service projects as needed, giving them the opportunity to work through the design or engineering process.

Passion Project PSAs

When students demonstrate passion for a topic, you can build on that with another short project: Students can create their own public service announcements (PSAs). For example, one of our elementary classes recently created posters to raise awareness about plastic straws and the effects they have on marine animals. They placed their posters at all of the restaurants near our beaches, encouraging patrons to "Skip the Straw." When students develop an interest in a cause, encourage them to create PSAs or other campaign materials that demonstrate their knowledge of the content you are learning, thereby encouraging steps toward change. Again, having a rubric and project guidelines ready at the beginning of the year will help make these opportunities happen. You can access a student movie-making rubric for self and peer review at **bit.ly/makingmoviesrubric**. Students may be capable of creating their own rubrics too, helping them develop a deeper understanding of content while practicing the Empowered Learner standard (ISTE Standards for Students, 2016).

Teaching Current Events

Allowing students the choice and opportunity to explore topics relevant to them increases engagement and learning outcomes, while making our classroom more enjoyable for everyone. Likewise, the Global Collaborator standard encourages students to "explore local and global issues and use collaborative technologies to work with others to investigate solutions" (ISTE Standards for Students, 7d, 2016). One way to engage students in this standard is by teaching current events. As Table 5.2 illustrates, you can incorporate current events and student interest topics in a variety of content area lessons, helping students connect to the world around them. Seeing these events through their eyes can be interesting and enlightening. Students often relate to events in different ways than adults and think of questions I never would have considered.

TABLE 5.2 TEACHING CURRENT EVENTS ACROSS CONTENT AREAS

LANGUAGE ARTS	MATH
• Students read current event articles and review text features and text structure. • Students choose a current event and list the who, what, when, where, and how. Next, they write a fictional story about characters that lived through that event. • After reading a current event news story, pose an opinion question to your students. This leads to a writing assignment, Socratic Seminar, or a class debate. • After reading the article, students engage in continued research to learn more about that event.	• Students analyze graphs and charts to solve real-world problems. Students create word problems based on information in an article or graph. • Teachers create real-world word problems for students to solve based on current events. • Pull facts from the news for students to graph, such as the number of endangered species left on the planet, or number of countries with female leaders. Students can create various types of graphs, including bar, line, and pictographs. Provide examples of these graphs in newspapers and other news sources (Hopkins, 2017).
SCIENCE	**SOCIAL STUDIES**
• After reading about a new species of animal, students research the habitat, adaptations, and characteristics of that animal. Students compare and contrast this new species with another animal. This works with plants as well. • After reading a current event article about a new invention, students work through the design process to improve that invention.	• Students choose a current event to compare and contrast with a historical event. This idea combines ELA research and writing with social studies concepts. • Students choose a historical event and find a current event or topic that is still affected by that event. For example: Find a current law or bill that is supported by the U.S. Constitution. • Students create a timeline to document how past events caused or impacted current events. For example, if students read about a new cell phone invention, they can research telephone inventions through history and create a timeline of those events. • Post a world, U.S., or state map on a bulletin board or use a digital map, such as Google Maps. Encourage students to research current event stories and place them on the map where the story took place, using string or digital pins (Hopkins, 2017).

INQUIRY AND WONDER WALL LESSONS

Incorporate spontaneity into your classroom by inviting students to research topics that make them curious. One great way to do this is with a Wonder Wall, a bulletin board or digital wall filled with sticky notes or posts with questions that stem from student curiosity. Whether sparked by a virtual or live field trip, a classroom experiment or simulation, or some other lesson or activities, these questions can lead to short research sessions that last one class period or less. Incorporating student-driven inquiry with a virtual reality (VR) or augmented reality (AR) tool, such as Google Expeditions (**edu.google.com/products/vr-ar/expeditions**), is a natural fit because students have so many questions as they engage with each scene of the immersive VR videos through their smartphone-based viewers. At first, students may need a little practice creating questions that are relevant to what you are studying, but usually by the end of the first session they catch on. (Lesson Plan 5.2 details how to implement virtual field trip inquiries.)

For a digital version of the Wonder Wall approach, you can use the website Wonderopolis (**wonderopolis.org**) for inquiry questions. This website has information about lots of questions students want answered, from "What is an amoeba?" to "Will AI replace human jobs?" to "What is bias and why do people have it?" and more. Students select a question, read the article, and conduct research on the topic. This can be presented in class or online using your learning management system (LMS).

Creating an Environment to Support Spontaneity

While we are each limited by the rules and restrictions set by our school or district, you can do a lot to create an environment conducive to creative projects and teachable moments—whether working with students in person or virtually.

The Flexible Classroom

When working to add spontaneity to your classroom, one important component is a flexible classroom environment. This means the ability to shift to small-group instruction and collaborative groups, as well to provide quiet areas for students to film and record audio. For example:

✦ Create individual and collaborative spaces. Consider your room and how you can set up zones for individual students to conduct research, record podcasts, and film or participate in videoconferences. Collaborative spaces need to be separate from the individual areas to prevent distractions. Hare and Dillon (2016) recommend observing students as they move through your space to examine traffic patterns and barriers to learning and collaborating. Take notes and consider what is needed to make your classroom work for the projects you are implementing. This should happen long before you buy new furniture, rugs, and the like. Survey students to ask their thoughts about design, color, and other learning space needs.

✦ Keep resources accessible. Classroom resources such as paper, craft supplies, and reference texts need to be visible and accessible to your students. Include sections of materials students can access freely and others that require permission. For example, glue dots are valuable when creating or building, but they are expensive and easily wasted. Another option is to create a digital catalog of all supplies available. These are things that teachers do not often consider when designing a classroom, but they can make a big impact on student creativity and choice.

✦ Take the learning outside. For a change of pace and to make the learning more memorable for students, prepare an outdoor learning space for those beautiful, sunny days. Figure 5.1 shows a small outdoor learning space my district designed for a kindergarten classroom. Students sit on tree stumps (ours were donated) and observe the vegetables growing in root viewers (built for around $200). Such a space can be great for students to explore nature, read, write, and engage in scientific investigations.

5.1 A kindergarten student captures a photo of a carrot growing in the school's root viewer.

Online Learning Content Curation Tools

Along with the physical setup of your learning space, consider how to prepare your online learning environment as well. Educators continually find new resources, briefly review them, and save them for later. Why not provide students with these same opportunities to curate content that interests them and can be explored more on a rainy day? This will require practice and scaffolding, but it is a great opportunity for students to continue their journey as lifelong learners. There are many tools students can use to help curate resources and research information they find. Here are a few of my favorites:

+ Padlet. A virtual bulletin board, Padlet (**padlet.com/dashboard**) allows you and your students to add messages, links, and videos, which is great for curation. You can organize your content in a variety of ways, from grids to concept maps. Free accounts offer only three boards, although paid subscriptions offer more.

+ Wakelet. You might recognize Wakelet (**wakelet.com**) as the newsletter template used by many educators and educational organizations, but it can also be used as a content curation tool, allowing students to create collections, invite collaborators, and save links and resources they find on the internet.

+ Microsoft OneNote. Like a virtual file cabinet, OneNote (**onenote.com**) contains notebooks, folders, and pages within it—only these pages can contain audio and video recordings too. You can monitor student notebooks and even write and record comments. OneNote also includes a Web Clipper extension for multiple browsers, making it easy to save links, graphics, and other files you find on the internet.

+ Google Docs or Microsoft Word. If you prefer to stick to basics, then students can use Google Docs (**docs.google.com**) or Microsoft Word online (**bit.ly/2DRljl9**) to curate information they find on the internet. This helps students organize content as they create a table of contents, add tables, and use other tools to group resources.

Exploring Data Analytics During Spontaneous Projects

The Computational Thinker standard 5a states that "students formulate problem definitions suited for technology-assisted methods such as data analysis, abstract models and algorithmic thinking in exploring and finding solutions" as well as "collect data or identify relevant data sets, use digital tools to analyze them, and represent data in various ways to facilitate problem-solving and decision-making" (ISTE Standards for Students, 5a and 5b, 2016). Problem solving, data analysis, and algorithmic thinking are all ways to incorporate math into your projects and fulfill these standards. Here are a few ideas for getting started:

✦ Google Applied Skills Courses. Google's Applied Skills training for students includes a course for data analytics and computational thinking: Pick the Next Box Office Hit (**bit.ly/2yrCA1J**) helps students begin analyzing data and trends in order to determine the next hit movie. This course was designed for high-school students, and it can be implemented at the beginning of the year to help prepare students to use these skills during projects.

✦ Google Trends. Google Trends (**trends.google.com**) is a useful website that provides time for short research projects stemming from questions, discussions, or debates during class. Students first search two or more topics using Google Trends, which then returns various types of data for students to evaluate in an attempt to identify trends and patterns. Short questions that require in-class research can assist students in honing their skills in a low-risk environment. For example, students can search renewable energy and nonrenewable energy and compare interest in those topics over time or in particular regions. This can lead to a discussion about why there is less interest in nonrenewable energy, or why there is more interest in renewable energy in certain regions.

✦ Science Journal. Available for iOS, Android, and Chromebook, the free Science Journal app (**sciencejournal.withgoogle.com**) is an *amazing* tool for student data analysis during science and math. Students use device sensors to locate light, sound, and movement, making comparisons and analyzing data while they perform hands-on and digital experiments.

LESSON PLANS

These lessons offer ways to add student choice and spontaneity into your classroom. You will notice they still incorporate standards in a meaningful way but add flexibility and choice to keep students engaged.

LESSON PLAN 5.1 Current Events Research Project

Subject: ELA/Science or Social Studies

Target Grades: 2–12

Duration: 1–2 class periods

Students research current events that align with content they are studying and provide an analysis demonstrating how a historical event or time period influenced the event. This lesson can be adapted for nearly any subject area, but it is most applicable in a social studies classroom.

Objectives

Grades 2–5 students will be able to:

✦ Conduct research to determine information about current events.

✦ Explain how perspective plays a role in how events are relayed.

✦ Explain how historical events affect events that occur today.

Grades 6–12 students will be able to:

✦ Conduct research, to compare, evaluate, and synthesize information about current events.

✦ Analyze primary and secondary sources to learn information about the past.

✦ Explain how perspective plays a role in how events are relayed.

✦ Explain how historical events affect events that occur today.

Standards Implemented in Lesson 5.1

ISTE STANDARDS FOR EDUCATORS	ISTE STANDARDS FOR STUDENTS	CONTENT AREA STANDARDS
Citizen 3b, 3c Designer 5b Facilitator 6a	Digital Citizen 2b, 2c Knowledge Constructor 3a, 3b, 3c, 3d Creative Communicator 6a, 6d Global Collaborator 7b, 7c	Students will engage in ELA research and informational reading standards, while learning about social studies/history concepts.

Preparation

Materials:

✦ Current events news source (Newsela, TweenTribune, or similar)

✦ Student content curation tool (Padlet, Wakelet, or similar)

✦ Polling tool (AnswerGarden, Poll Everywhere, or similar)

Instructions

 Use a tool such as AnswerGarden or Poll Everywhere to generate a survey word cloud with your class. Ask each student what word or short phrase comes to mind when they think of the news. As students respond, the answers submitted most frequently will be displayed larger in the cloud. Use this word cloud to begin a short discussion on news, primary sources, bias, and alternative perspectives. Ask students where they look to find local or global news.

 Share the news sources in your LMS, or in an online tool such as Padlet, and provide students time to preview them.

Divide students into groups of two to four, asking them to research current events that were caused/affected by or related to a historical event. Provide some examples, such as how the U.S. Constitution influences current laws or how the Dust Bowl of the 1930s relates to current similar events due to climate change. Another example is Alexander Hamilton's contribution to The Federalist Papers and how they informed presidential impeachment hearings in recent years.

Students work with their teammates using an online document to locate relevant articles and begin searching for news sources that provide alternative viewpoints and perspectives. They may use a videoconference tool to discuss their research.

Students create a Then and Now project of their choice, such as a collage, presentation, video, PSA, or any other medium to present their findings.

Students present their project in an online LMS discussion or Padlet wall. They could also present face-to-face through a Speed Dating activity in which students rotate from classmate to classmate, taking turns sharing their short presentations. Speed Dating works best if each presentation is only 2–3 minutes in length.

Extensions

Use the student presentations for a Socratic Seminar, which typically involves organizing students into a circle (or a virtual circle in a videoconference) for an organized discussion focused on open-ended questions about a text, video, or other source. The teacher will ask questions to help students dig deeper into the causes and consequences of historical and current events.

ONLINE AND REMOTE LEARNING ADAPTATION

The teacher explains the project during a videoconference session and then prompts students to conduct their research online. If working in groups, students can use an online document to collaborate and curate information. Students create their presentation, video, or other multimedia product to share their findings and host their completed product in Flipgrid, their LMS, or another tool such as Padlet. The Socratic Seminar extension lesson can be completed using an online platform such as Tricider or Parlay, allowing students to engage in an online discussion.

LESSON PLAN 5.2 Inquiry Expeditions

Subject: Science, ELA Research

Target Grades: K–12

Duration: 1 class period

Students engage in the inquiry process while interacting with Google Expeditions or another virtual field trip platform. Later, students will conduct research to learn more about the questions they were unable to answer during the virtual field trip. I created this lesson after facilitating numerous Google Expeditions with students using smartphone-based VR headsets. They were really engaged; however, the lessons neglected to help them think critically or apply the information they learned. By adding inquiry to these experiences, students are given a choice in what they learn and research, and they are continuously asking themselves questions about what they see as they engage in the virtual tours.

Standards Implemented in Lesson 5.2

ISTE STANDARDS FOR EDUCATORS	ISTE STANDARDS FOR STUDENTS	CONTENT AREA STANDARDS
Citizen 3b, 3c Designer 5b Facilitator 6a	Digital Citizen 2b, 2c Knowledge Constructor 3a, 3b Global Collaborator 7c	Students will engage in science observation and content standards, practicing their inquiry skills. Students will use ELA information reading and research standards to gather additional information about their topic.

Objectives

Grades K–5 students will be able to:

✦ Create inquiry questions about things they are curious about or wonder.

✦ Answer their own inquiry questions from viewing content and/or conducting additional research.

✦ Interpret and evaluate the information they research.

Grades 6–12 students will be able to:

✦ Ask inquiry questions to help define a problem and think critically about what they are learning.

✦ Answer their own inquiry questions from viewing content and/or conducting additional research.

✦ Interpret, evaluate, and synthesize the information they research.

Preparation

Materials:

✦ Google Expeditions app on a mobile device or Chrome OS.

✦ Optional: Google Cardboard or other compatible VR headset

Instructions

 Inform students that they will be going on a virtual field trip with Google Expeditions (or similar platform). Explain the location and ask students to discuss what they already know about this topic. Next, provide students with small whiteboards or clipboards with paper. Display the first scene in the expedition, allowing students to explore on their own. Next, ask students to think of inquiry questions, things they are wondering about the topic. On a shared display, ask students to explain their questions. Write these questions and discuss which ones make good inquiry questions. Explain that good inquiry questions are relevant to the topic, encourage students to dig deeper and think (they can't be answered yes, no, or a single word), and are questions they genuinely want to learn about.

Next, read the script associated with that scene, then pause to allow students to begin answering their inquiry questions. Move to the next scene, but this time allow students to create their own inquiry questions on their whiteboards (Figure 5.2). Continue this process as students write questions and try to answer them as they explore each scene.

5.2 While they participate in a virtual field trip, students write inquiry questions.

At the end of the expedition, students determine which questions still need to be answered. Provide time for students to conduct research to find additional answers to the questions. Students write their answers in an LMS or other discussion forum.

 The teacher relates the content learned to previous content and addresses any misconceptions or errors in reasoning that were posted in the online discussions.

Extensions

The inquiry research could lead to passion projects that allow students to research topics that interest them, such as a campaign to petition for sustainable lunch trays, or research about a place they would like to visit. Later, students create projects related to these interests.

ONLINE AND REMOTE LEARNING ADAPTATION

The teacher posts the virtual field trip or Google Expedition link in the LMS or similar platform for students to access. Students view the virtual field trip on their devices and engage in the inquiry process. Students post their questions in a discussion, allowing peers and the teacher to provide feedback and identify questions that help students gain a deeper understanding of the content. Students begin answering the questions with content from the field trip or expedition and conduct research to gain information about any unanswered questions. Students will post their responses in the discussion forum.

LESSON PLAN 5.3 Improv Presentations

Subject: Any

Target Grades: 2–12

Duration: 1–2 class periods

Improv presentations are an effective way to ensure that students truly understand the content they are presenting, rather than reading bullet points in their slideshow. Students will engage in the research process, learning more about a topic. However, instead of students creating a presentation based on their research, the teacher displays random photos on the screen and students improvise a talk, relating their content back to the information they researched. The idea is to give the illusion that the slides are part of a prepared presentation, similar to how a professional would. This can help prepare students for other spontaneous events, such as career and college interviews—or being asked to speak to clients or coworkers about a company project on the spur of the moment.

Objectives

Grades 2–12 students will be able to:

+ Conduct effective research about a topic.

+ Effectively communicate information they learned about a topic, using analogies and other types of comparisons.

Preparation

Materials:

+ Presentation software (Google Slides, Microsoft PowerPoint, Keynote, Buncee, or similar)

Advanced Preparation:

✦ Find random, interesting photos and create a slideshow with the images. Resist the urge to find photos that match your topic, as the goal is for students to improvise a comparison between the topic and something unrelated. You may need to create a different slideshow for each class period.

✦ Alternatively, ask students to submit photos and compile these into the slideshow.

Standards Implemented in Lesson 5.3

ISTE STANDARDS FOR EDUCATORS	ISTE STANDARDS FOR STUDENTS	CONTENT AREA STANDARDS
Citizen 3b, 3c Designer 5b Facilitator 6a	Digital Citizen 2b, 2c Knowledge Constructor 3a, 3b Creative Communicator 6d Global Collaborator 7c	Students will dig deeper into content topics while also using ELA standards and speaking and listening skills to conduct and present research.

Instructions

Explain the improv presentations to students. It may be a good idea to practice this at the end of a couple class periods, asking students to participate in an improv to summarize the content provided in class that day. Demonstrate improv with your students by asking them to provide you with a topic. Display a slideshow with a few random photos and demonstrate how you can "present" about that topic using the slideshow. Divide students into groups to begin researching their topics. Improv can be used for science body systems, life cycles, world explorers, historical events, or any other content.

Provide time for students to begin researching and taking notes. Remind them that their goal is to present essential information about their topic, so they may want to divide some of the content standards or topic information among their group members, similar to a Jigsaw presentation. Students can use a videoconference tool, online document, or both to collaborate and curate their research.

 Provide time for student presentations. Although these could be presented online, part of the fun is the fact that it is a spontaneous shared event, so I recommend a face-to-face setting for these types of presentations.

 Provide time for students to reflect and ask questions in an online discussion in your LMS or other platform.

Extensions

Combine the improv approach with Lesson Plan 6.2 to provide students with opportunities to fact-check other presentations and engage in conversations or debates about concepts. With improv, it is likely students will accidentally present some misconceptions or inaccurate information as they try to recall the content they researched, so this is an effective way to correct some of these errors.

ONLINE AND REMOTE LEARNING ADAPTATION

The spontaneity of this project is best suited for a synchronous classroom environment, whether in a brick-and-mortar or an online classroom. During a videoconference session in a platform such as Zoom or Google Meet, you could screenshare slideshows of random photos and then have students take turns presenting live. Another option is to send students the slideshow and ask them to screen-record themselves giving their presentation, but this would allow students to preview the photos or create multiple edits if they make mistakes.

COACH'S CONNECTION

Spontaneity and analysis may seem like the opposite ends of a spectrum, but they actually require similar skills: the ability to comprehend meaning and take action in the face of unexpected data. This chapter explored these skills from both perspectives. To engage students in incorporating spontaneity into lessons and projects, which requires students to be adept at content curation, teachers need to be competent themselves. So, this Coach's Connection provides effective ways to incorporate this skill into your coaching. This chapter also offered ideas for incorporating data analysis into projects, which is a great opportunity to explore the Computational Thinking standard (ISTE Standards for Students, 2016). Teachers often struggle with this standard, making it a great opportunity to step in as a coach.

Collaborative Curation

Collaboration is key for coaches, both with sharing resources and ideas with our PLNs and in our work with teachers. One characteristic successful coaches have in common is that they view teachers as collaborative partners, working together to create valuable and engaging experiences for their students. The Collaborator standard emphasizes this skill, stating that coaches "partner with educators to evaluate the efficacy of digital learning content and tools to inform procurement decisions and adoption" (ISTE Standards for Coaches, 3c, 2019).

A way to incorporate this standard into our daily practice is through shared resources with the teachers we coach. Using your district LMS, Padlet, OneNote, or another tool of your choice, begin curating lists of district-approved resources and gaining valuable feedback from educators. To kick off this initiative, I recommend taking the following actions:

✦ Gather a diverse group of educators to begin establishing criteria for evaluating websites, programs, apps, and digital curriculum. They may suggest categories such as usability, student engagement, product support, and educational value. Try to direct teachers to create general categories that can apply to any app, website, or learning resource. I have found that no matter how long I test out a new resource, teachers always find something I missed or want to use the tool in a way I never considered. To make this project useful, gather feedback from the beginning and ensure that teachers feel comfortable using the platform you select. A bonus is that you already have a group of teachers who will spread the word to others and encourage their colleagues to submit evaluations as well.

✦ Consider how you would like your finished, curated content site to look and how much time you plan to spend on the initiative. One option is to use Padlet, allowing teachers to comment using the categories your group selected. If you prefer the published guide to be more polished, teachers can submit evaluations using a Google Forms or Microsoft Forms document. Then they can aggregate their data into a website or document that is updated as new evaluations are submitted or resources are updated.

✦ Reach out to your curriculum team and school administrators prior to beginning this project. This is coming from personal experience in which I enthusiastically launched projects and events on my own, later realizing that I could have benefited from their help and support. Their support will also help create buy-in from educators.

✦ Consider how you will acknowledge teachers for their time and work. This can be as simple as providing credit for their input and ideas on your website or earning a digital badge.

Coaching to Promote Computational Thinking

When reflecting on the ISTE Standards for Students (2016), I noticed many teachers list Computational Thinker as one they find most challenging. This is both in their understanding of what computational thinking actually is and in ideas for its implementation. To help teachers gain a better understanding of computational thinking and what it looks like in their grade levels, try these ideas:

+ Define computational thinking. During professional learning events, start by forming a definition of computational thinking. Provide time for teachers to conduct some research (2–3 minutes) and then discuss the meaning with their groups. Each group can engage in a Speed Dating sharing session, in which they continually modify their definition based on ideas shared from other groups. I feel that when teachers see others wrestling with the meaning, they will find more comfort in asking questions and understanding that it is okay to have a slightly different interpretation than the teacher next door.

+ Engage the experts. If this is not your area of expertise, partner with some math, science, or STEM teachers to help create some examples of what computational thinking can look like at various grade levels. You can task high school students with creating lessons to share with elementary students, for instance (see Lesson Plan 4.2 for ideas).

+ Share online resources. One excellent online resource is Kathy Schrock's Guide to Everything (**bit.ly/321lzb4**), which offers lesson plans, ideas, and references to promote computational thinking. ISTE also provides numerous resources and articles to support computational thinking skills. Visit **bit.ly/istecomputationalthinking** to access these materials. Together, coaches and educators can highlight these examples by bringing in face-to-face and virtual guest speakers, creating book displays of careers and people who regularly engage in computational thinking, or provide student projects to engage in career-focused concepts.

Engage Students to Set and Track Their Own Goals

The Data-Driven Decision-Maker standard explains that "coaches partner with educators to empower students to use learning data to set their own goals and measure their progress" (ISTE Standards for Coaches, 6c, 2019). Goal setting is beneficial when implementing projects and for students to track their own progress on assessments, writing, and other assignments. Students' goal-setting and progress-measuring abilities will vary depending on their grade level, but students can begin tracking their math and reading fluency data and analyzing it to determine patterns as early as kindergarten. I love the idea of incorporating this with reflection. For example, after taking an assessment, students write how they studied that week, how much they studied, what time of day they took the assessment, their mood that day, and so on. This can be provided in survey format using Google Forms or Microsoft Forms. Students can use quantitative data (amounts, percents, graphs), along with qualitative data (journal entries, photographs) to begin creating progress goals, as well as detailed plans for how to achieve those goals.

One way to encourage progress tracking is to incorporate data notebooks into your classroom. Whether paper or digital, these notebooks are filled with student fluency data, and stickers or digital icons to place on their graphs as they achieve goals. Students include their goals for the year and portfolio-level work they are proud to display. Students can also use Google Sheets or the PicCollage EDU app to display their data and goals. An alternative is for students to record their own video or audio clips explaining their goals and progress. Goals are especially useful during projects, in which students can get sidetracked by design elements or irrelevant content. Checking goals and data regularly will help students stay focused on what they need to know in order to reach mastery.

In middle and high school, students can take this a step further, creating algorithms and using conditional formatting and code to find patterns and delve deeper into their data. The Empowered Learner standard encourages students to "articulate and set personal learning goals, develop strategies leveraging technology to achieve them and reflect on the learning process itself to improve learning outcomes" (ISTE Standards for Students, 1a, 2016). Along with tracking their own academic data, students can use spreadsheets and algorithmic thinking to analyze progress in projects they are working on in their classes.

Help Teachers Use Computational Thinking for Data Collection

What better way to help educators become more comfortable with computational thinking than to begin implementing it in their own work. Here are two ideas to help you encourage this that may be fun to implement in your own coaching practice as well.

+ Google Analytics Academy. The Google Analytics Academy (**analytics.google.com/analytics/academy**) offers courses for adults to begin learning how to implement data analytics in their careers. While not designed or geared toward educators, these courses can help teachers begin to gain a better understanding of how data analytics can work for them and how to incorporate analytics in their career-focused authentic projects.

+ Google Sheets Explore Tool. The Explore tool is one of my favorite features available in Google Sheets. To access this feature, open a sheet filled with data and, in the bottom-right corner, click the squarish icon with a star inside. The Explore tool enables you to ask questions about your data. So if you are not certain which formula to use, ask the question and Google will answer it *and* provide the formula you could have used. This is perfect for those who are not comfortable using spreadsheet formulas and also for those who want to expand their skills or work more efficiently. This feature also allows you to apply conditional formatting easily and provides some sample graphs for you to use.

 So what spontaneous memories are you making in your classroom? I look forward to hearing about them on Twitter under the hashtag #AuthenticEdVentures.

MAKE THE MOST OF YOUR TIME

If *Family Feud* asked 100 teachers to name the biggest barrier to engaging students in projects, the survey would say *"Time!"* is the top answer. Time gets in the way for so many reasons, from impossible pacing guides to impromptu fire drills to playground or relationship drama that interrupts lessons. Fitting everything in becomes nearly impossible. While not a miracle solution, this chapter will provide tips and strategies for project time management and making the most of the time you have with your students.

To create lifelong learners and students who will remember what we taught for many years to come, we need to explore standards in depth, which is best achieved in authentic and relevant lessons, and these, in turn, need time. We may not fit in everything, but if we cram in more simply for the sake of checking requirements off a list, will students remember it after the summer anyway? We know they will not, which is why districts and schools create schedules to ensure that important exams take place before long breaks. They are certain that students will forget everything they learned by the time they return. Then what is the point?

GOALS, REMINDERS, AND INSPIRATION

To help you stay focused, consider creating reminders about the important goals and skills you want students to gain by the end of the year. This can help relieve anxiety when you get stressed about the time that got away, refocusing you on the key skills and concepts you want students to take with them at the end of the year. For example, you could try:

+ Inspirational Decor. Why not have your decor work for you and your students, and place messages around the room to remind you of your class mission and goals? From vinyl decals and painted walls to pencils, pillows, and more, one of my favorite aspects of being a coach is getting to view numerous classrooms with their unique decor and inspirational messages. In an online course, you can include inspirational quotes and memes in LMS folders or online content to help motivate students throughout the year.

✦ Unexpected Notes. Another fun option is to leave yourself unexpected messages either with sticky notes on random planner pages or through scheduled emails. The unexpected is often more memorable than things we plan, so these messages can serve as a great reminder of our goals. FutureMe (**Futureme.org**) enables you to schedule emails to yourself in the future, for example. Microsoft Outlook and Gmail also have options for scheduling emails. However, paper cards and sticky notes embedded in lesson plan books are just as effective.

✦ Reflective Journals. Digital or paper journals can help you and your students reflect on what is important and how they are working to become lifelong learners. Some short prompts might help get thoughts rolling. For example, "What is something you want to learn how to do? How can you find out more?" Or, "Describe something meaningful you did this week. How can you continue this in the coming days or weeks?"

✦ Time to Ponder. Set aside time to consider your goals. Just 3 to 5 minutes per day can make an impact and help you refocus when the world is calling for you to do what is urgent versus what is important. I set "do not disturb" on my phone and laptop because it is so easy to get distracted by life.

TIME MANAGEMENT

I have yet to meet a teacher who is happy with the amount of time they are allotted to complete their planning and lessons. Although I don't have an extra hour to lend you, I do have some suggestions that might make lessons somewhat more manageable and productive when implementing projects. Some focus on managing time efficiently, while others focus more on making the most of your time with students. Considering both will help make projects more manageable and enjoyable.

Daniel H. Pink, author of *When: The Scientific Secrets of Perfect Timing*, researched which time of day is best for certain activities. For example, in a keynote I attended, he stated that 4:00 p.m. to 8:00 p.m. is the best time to engage in brainstorming and divergent thinking (Pink, 2020). I wondered how this science of timing might be applied in classrooms. You could, for example, begin to track patterns in your own classrooms. Set aside a few days for this and survey students to determine when they feel the most alert, tired, overwhelmed, or antsy. Observe students and track their non-verbal behavior clues. From this data, you can adjust your schedule to make the most of time when students are most productive. If we can "hack" our schedules to create the highest-possible productivity, then we have time to accomplish more with our students.

Create a Sense of Urgency

Another way to increase productivity is by creating a sense of urgency while students are creating projects and working through tasks. According to Ormrod and Jones (2018), some stress can actually be a good thing. Think about it: Would *Candy Crush* or *Tetris* be as much fun without time limits? Providing deadlines, using timers, and including other classroom management strategies to promote a sense of urgency can actually increase productivity in some situations.

For example, one strategy to help promote a sense of urgency in students is called Show Me. When initiating a task or project, inform students the amount of time to complete the task and set a timer. Be conservative and set the timer for an amount that only the fastest students will achieve. Then give regular time updates, stating, "Three more minutes," and then "One more minute." When the alarm goes off, ask students to "show me" using their fingers how much more time they think they need. Again, set the timer for one of the lower amounts suggested by student hands, and start the process over. This allows students and groups to become more aware of deadlines and learn that teachers and other students are relying on them to finish.

You can also prompt a sense of urgency by assigning a student to be the "timer" during tasks. This student is responsible for setting a timer and helping keep teammates focused. Particularly in elementary school, students take this job seriously. One note, though, is that this might make the student timer focus more on the timing device and less on the project itself. For this reason, I prefer the Show Me strategy.

Combine Standards and Content Areas

Another effective way to save time in your classroom is by combining standards and content areas in your projects and lessons. You will be amazed at how many standards can fit well in one lesson when you take a little time to plan. Students begin to see authentic applications for concepts they are learning and have multiple attempts throughout the year to master each standard.

Time-Management Tools and Strategies

When engaging students in project-based learning, another way to save time and monitor progress is with task management tools and strategies. Task management serves many purposes in the classroom, including:

+ Helping students meet project milestones and deadlines

+ Helping teachers monitor student progress and assist those who are off track or falling behind

+ Helping students see how their work affects others and how other tasks are dependent on their contributions

+ Helping teachers grade fairly, while ensuring that tasks are clearly explained for each student (for example, deducting points only from students who complete faulty research or plagiarism rather than the whole group)

Project-management tools and strategies help students develop a sense of urgency and maintain project deadlines, eliminating last-minute rushing and procrastination. When we rush through a project to "get it finished," we teach students that this is an acceptable way to work. Rather, let's teach them about the importance of practice and iteration, as well as the value of reflection. The following sections provide task management ideas and tools that are beneficial for a variety of grade levels and project types.

Project To Do Lists

Creating digital To Do task boards for your students will serve several purposes during class projects. These small tasks help break up the larger project and keep students from becoming overwhelmed. Digital boards allow students to work on their projects at home and make updates from anywhere at any time. Using the task board shown in Figure 6.1, for example, you would assign tasks for students in the To Do List column, then have students move their tasks to the In Progress column when they begin working. Students move the task to the Group Check column next, and group members review their work. If all group members agree, then they move that task to the Teacher Check column, and you can either move that task to Completed or back to In Progress if revisions still need to be made. If your students are skilled at working cooperatively, you can allow them to divide the tasks amongst themselves.

Here are a few platforms that that will help you implement digital To Do lists with students:

✦ Microsoft OneNote. If you are using OneNote Class Notebook (**onenote.com/classnotebook**) with your students already, then this is a great option for digital To Do lists. You can add a table in OneNote and allow students to type tasks in each column. All group members have access to the notebook and are able to add typed and audio comments for feedback.

+ Google Slides and Google Docs. Google Slides (**slides.google.com**) and Google Docs (**docs.google.com**) can also be used for student To Do lists. Adding a table with text boxes allows students to add and assign tasks to group members while you monitor their progress.

+ Padlet. A virtual bulletin board website, Padlet (**padlet.com**) offers a To Do list template, making it easy to set up tasks and monitor each group. Students and teachers can add audio or video feedback.

+ Scrumy. Scrumy (**scrumy.com**) is a website created for To Do list task management. It is easy to use and does not require student accounts.

+ Trello. The task management tool Trello (**trello.com**) allows teams to prioritize tasks, add tags, and assign tasks and due dates to group members. The free version allows up to 10 team boards.

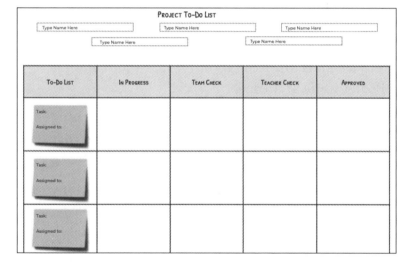

6.1 You can download and modify the To Do List Template (**bit.ly/3iMfDsu**) to work for your projects and students.

Looking at the example in Figure 6.1, you begin to see how students engage in an iterative process that designers and other professionals use every day. This process allows students to practice the Empowered Learner standard: "Students use technology to seek feedback that informs and improves their practice and to demonstrate their learning in a variety of ways" (ISTE Standards for Students, 1c, 2016).

Check-in Journals

If digital To Do lists seem daunting, then consider a less intense approach to project management. Check-in Journals are a variation of agile project management used by software developers that incorporate daily check-ins to ensure that all team members are focused and informed about progress updates.

Using an online discussion board, periodically ask students to stop what they are doing and write down their progress that class period. This is a great strategy when students start losing focus, or when an administrator walks in and your organized chaos is looking more chaotic than organized. I find that students who were off-task typically write what they should have been doing and then get back on track. This eliminates the need to nag or scold students, and instead helps them take steps toward self-regulation. To implement Check-in Journals, you could use:

✦ Padlet. Padlet is a great tool if you are comfortable with students having access to each other's journals. Keep in mind that the free version allows only three Padlet walls at a time.

✦ Any LMS. Whether you use Schoology, Canvas, or another learning management system, students can respond to a discussion or assignment with their journal response.

✦ Paper Journals. Yes, it is okay to use paper sometimes! Some of my favorite projects blend paper or hands-on learning with technology. Students can snap a picture and share it with classmates and teachers.

Project Checklists

Another tool that works well, particularly with elementary students, is a project checklist (Figure 6.2). Checklists are easier than rubrics for younger students, helping break the project into smaller tasks with deadlines. Students need approval for each section, ensuring that they do not miss important steps, and mistakes are caught early.

Human Body Student Checklist

How do the organs in our bodies help us to stay healthy, grow, and perform daily tasks?

Checklist	✔
• Include at least 6 facts in our riddle.	
• Checked our riddle to make sure the facts are not too easy to guess.	
• Checked our riddle to make sure we included detailed and unique facts. *(see below)*	
• Facts are written in our own words (not copied and pasted).	
• We wrote our riddle and it was approved by our teacher.	
• We created a Google Slide for our riddle.	

6.2 Project checklists are useful to keep students on track, particularly in younger grades.

Gantt Charts

A more advanced project-management tool to use with students, Gantt charts create a project timeline with tasks and dependencies (Figure 6.3). For example, if you are painting a room, you need to prime first. If shipping for the primer is delayed, that sets back your entire project because you are unable to move forward until the primer is applied and dry. When this occurs, the Gantt chart will automatically redistribute the complete timeline, showing you how much your project is delayed. In a professional setting, project managers typically add slack or float time to the project to account for these delays. Gantt charts are a great way to help middle- and high-school students understand how important it is to complete tasks on time (although I would not count out elementary classes either). These charts also help create a sense of urgency as students work through tasks.

Unlike student To Do lists, free online Gantt chart programs that are kid-friendly can be difficult to find. Kanbanchi (**kanbanchi.com**) currently offers free project-management tools for educators, including Gantt charts, and TeamGantt (**teamgantt.com**) allows one free Gantt chart for groups of three or less, as well as a free Google Sheets template (**bit.ly/3bUyo8B**). Although you'll need to add the dependencies to the template manually, it is still a great introduction to Gantt charts and more advanced task and project management. You also can create your own chart fairly easily, but you would need to update timeline delays manually.

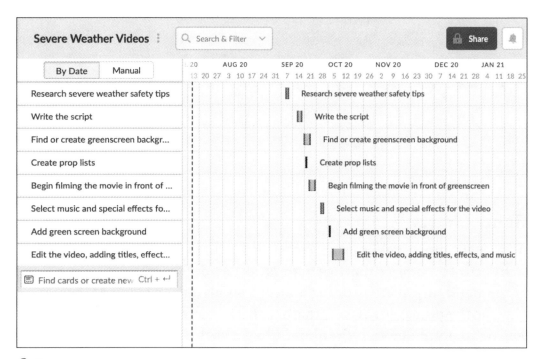

6.3 A Gantt chart not only shows the tasks and timeline for a project but can also illustrate how a delay at one step affects subsequent project steps.

Project and Interval Timers

Timers are helpful tools to use during projects. They help teachers and students maintain deadlines and work more efficiently. Beyond the digital and online timers you may already use, you can try interval timers. Interval timers are typically used for exercise workouts, but you can hack them to help with classroom management during station rotations or student project presentations. One of my favorite interval timer sites is **intervaltimer.com**, which enables you to determine the number of rounds (presentation rotations), the amount of time in each round, and transition time. Some apps include alarms and reminders to inform students when the round is ending. These timers allow you to focus on the student learning and presentations, rather than time management.

ENGAGING THE AUDIENCE DURING PRESENTATIONS

My biggest complaint with traditional classroom presentations is how little interaction the student audience has with the presenter. While I definitely think there should be time set aside for students to learn how to be audience members, this can be reserved for assemblies, guest speakers, and field trips to the symphony. During classroom presentations, we need students actively learning, increasing their engagement and retention of information. The following sections provide ways to add more interaction to student presentations and to make the most of students' time while they are audience members. (In addition, Lesson Plan 6.2 details yet another type of interactive presentation.)

Elaboration Strategy

The learning sciences demonstrate brain-based strategies that are scientifically proven as effective to promote retention of information (Hoadley, 2018). One strategy, *elaboration*, encourages students to ask questions as they read or listen to information, and then try to answer them as the video, book, or presentation continues. In other words, rather than asking students merely to take notes during a presentation, you ask students to use elaboration and write down questions that occur to them as they listen. For example, if one student presents about endangered species in Florida, a classmate may wonder, "How did they become endangered?" or "How can we help this species survive?" Students write down these questions and then try to answer them during the presentation. With younger students, pause and provide time to answer their questions. Elaboration and other learning science strategies are ways not only to trick ourselves into paying attention but also to add more interactivity into presentations.

Role-Playing Presentations

The role-playing strategy tasks students with researching a character and then playing that part during an activity or presentation. Students respond to historic reenactments and questions in a way they feel their character would. You can facilitate a role-playing lesson in two ways.

In the first type, all students participate as a character without audience members. You could organize this as a face-to-face session or virtually in a chat or discussion board. You can also use an app such as ChatterPix Kids (**bit.ly/2Xxwx52**) for students to respond to a question, and then create other responses to other characters' posts. Think of it as a debate but with role-playing thrown in as well.

Another way to do this is to split the class into two groups. Half role-play as their characters, while the others are audience members who ask questions, such as "Why did you choose to participate in the strike?" In answering, the role-playing student must provide evidence to explain why their character took that action. The groups then swap roles so that everyone has a chance to role-play and ask questions. Again, this could be done as a face-to-face session or virtually. The virtual version is easier to grade, but both would be fun ways to engage your entire class and ensure that students really know their content.

Try Online Video Presentations

Think about how much presentations have evolved in the career world. In the last few months alone, I used online communication to plan conference sessions with distant colleagues, watched tutorials for professional and personal projects, and attended webinars to learn more about educational products and strategies. Your online activity is probably similar to this, as it is for many of our students as well. If online and video presentations are helpful in our lives outside the classroom, why not bring them inside the classroom?

Hosting presentations online will save a tremendous amount of class time as well. In a typical classroom, getting through everyone's presentations might take up to four days. If students are not working cooperatively, it could be even longer. With an online format, students can be assigned presentations to peer review during learning stations or as homework. They can then provide feedback through discussions, audio comments, or online forms. Not only does this approach free up class time, but it also increases student interactivity as audience members. In addition, online presentations can be as short as 30 seconds and might be less formal than what we think of as a classroom report—a good activity to combine with those unexpected teachable moments.

The lesson plans included in this chapter detail ways to help students engage in online presentations. In addition to these, however, I encourage you to provide opportunities for students to create shorter and less rehearsed presentations, along with increased opportunities for online communication. Videos are a great forum for this.

Tutorial videos are also a perfect fit to integrate projects regularly during math lessons. Providing students with an option to create videos allows them to explore content vocabulary, as well as demonstrate their reasoning and thinking while solving a problem. The Common Core State Standards of Mathematical Practice for grades K–12 include the following strategies:

+ Make sense of problems and persevere in solving them.

+ Reason abstractly and quantitatively.

+ Construct viable arguments and critique the reasoning of others.

+ Model with mathematics.

+ Use appropriate tools strategically.

+ Attend to precision.

+ Look for and make use of structure.

+ Look for and express regularity in repeated reasoning. (CPALMS, 2020)

Even if you do not use the Common Core State Standards in your school, these are great skills to include in math lessons (see Lesson Plan 2.4 for more ideas).

These videos help encourage self-regulation, make the station more fun for students, and provide more entertainment for students as they watch their classmates' videos. For example, students can begin their video by stating, "Hi friends, today we are going to talk about fractions. All fractions have a numerator (*student holds up photo booth prop with the word* numerator)." Students continue the video explaining the vocabulary word and solving the problem of the day. This 5–10-minute activity takes the same amount of time as a traditional problem-solving station, after an initial orientation to teach students how to create videos. Additionally, teachers can easily identify errors in student reasoning and provide examples of multiple strategies for solving problems.

Another way to implement informal presentations in your classroom is through Just in Time student support videos. In your LMS or another platform, begin a discussion where students can pose questions they struggle to answer. Then allow other students to respond to the discussion with their own short tutorial videos. Students can earn extra points for creating videos and assisting their classmates, and the activity will help build confidence in their abilities. Those in need of help will receive timely feedback from peers explaining concepts in a relatable way.

LESSON PLANS

The following lesson plans feature some time-management tools and ideas discussed in this chapter. You will notice Check-in Journals, the Show Me strategy, and digital To Do lists used to help monitor students.

LESSON PLAN 6.1 Virtual Field Trips

Subject: Any content area

Target Grades: K–12

Duration: 1–2 weeks

Student-created virtual field trips are an effective way to ensure that students are engaged while visiting local landmarks and venues during their in-person field trips. There are numerous ways to do this, and this project can be implemented in any grade level. During the field trip, students take pictures, make notes, and record audio of their tour. When they return to school, students create hyperlinked tours of their experience (Figure 6.4). These tours are shared with other classes around the world or other grade levels in their own district.

6.4 Using Google Slides, students can create a virtual field trip with hyperlinks.

Objectives

Grades K–12 students will be able to:

✦ Explain their knowledge of content standards.

✦ Create and share presentations, adapting the message for their intended audience.

Standards Implemented in Lesson 6.1

ISTE STANDARDS FOR EDUCATORS	ISTE STANDARDS FOR STUDENTS	CONTENT AREA STANDARDS
Citizen 3c Designer 5b Facilitator 6a	Digital Citizen 2b, 2c Knowledge Constructor 3a Creative Communicator 6d Global Collaborator 7c	Students will create presentations to help them focus on content standards while attending a class field trip. Students will practice ELA writing standards while creating a presentation that is clear and includes proper grammar and formatting.

Preparation

Materials:

✦ Cameras, smartphones, or iPads

✦ Note-taking materials or audio recorder

✦ Presentation tool (Microsoft PowerPoint, Google Slides, Keynote, Buncee, or similar)

✦ Virtual Field Trip Student Checklist (**bit.ly/3d1CywB**)

✦ Alligator Farm Example (**bit.ly/2X2GWWR**)

Advanced Preparation:

✦ Show students the Virtual Field Trip Student Checklist.

✦ Discuss expectations prior to attending the field trip.

Instructions

 Display an example of a student virtual field trip. Show students the checklist or rubric for the assignment. Divide students into groups to review the field trip tour. If possible, provide students with a map of the location and the exhibits you will be visiting. Provide time for students to make a plan for the field trip and presentation.

 During the field trip, students take photographs, video clips, and notes.

 When students return from the trip, demonstrate how to create hyperlinks in their slides, allowing choices and inter-activity for those viewing the slideshow.

 Provide students time to upload and organize their content, create their slideshows, and conduct additional research.

 Provide students time to finalize their virtual field trip. While students create their virtual field trips, use the Show Me strategy to determine how much more time each group needs. Use Check-in Journals, asking students to relay their progress.

 Provide time for students to peer review their classmates' slides using Padlet or an online discussion board.

  Display the slideshows on a website or in your LMS. Students can present their slideshows live for other classes.

Extensions

Google Tour Creator (**arvr.google.com/tourcreator**) offers a way for students to create their own Google Expeditions. Students will need a 360° camera or the Google Street View app to take 360° photos. When students return from their field trip, they upload photos to the Google Tour Creator app and create their tours. These tours can be viewed on Google Poly (**poly.google.com**) or with VR headsets and a mobile device on the Google Expeditions app.

ONLINE AND REMOTE LEARNING ADAPTATION

Students participate in a virtual tour of a location or schedule a videoconference with someone who works in a museum, national park, or other relevant location. While observing the virtual field trip, students take notes and create recordings. Students use videoconference tools and an online document to collaborate and create their virtual field trip. Students can also create a virtual field trip after visiting a local landmark or attraction near their homes. For younger students, this could be as simple as a task that asks students to "Find five things that start with the letter H." With older students, tasks such as "Find evidence of the Industrial Revolution in your town" could result in some creative virtual tours.

LESSON PLAN 6.2 Tell Me Something I Don't Know

Subject: ELA/Any other content area

Target Grades: 4–12

Duration: 2–3 class periods

This project was inspired by the podcast *Tell Me Something I Don't Know* with Stephen J. Dubner of Freakonomics Radio. In the show, presenters try to "wow" judges with interesting and unique information. The podcast includes judges who assess the information based on the following:

+ Is it true?

+ Is it interesting information?

+ Is it something the judges truly didn't know?

Standards Implemented in Lesson 6.2

ISTE STANDARDS FOR EDUCATORS	ISTE STANDARDS FOR STUDENTS	CONTENT AREA STANDARDS
Citizen 3b, 3c Designer 5b Facilitator 6a	Digital Citizen 2b, 2c Knowledge Constructor 3a, 3b, 3d Creative Communicator 6d Global Collaborator 7c	Students will use ELA standards to conduct research and assess the validity of content and sources. Students will gain a deeper understanding of content standards.

Along with judges, live fact-checkers are available to verify that the information is true, and the judges vote on their favorite presentation.

In the classroom, this content would relate back to standards and units in a particular course. The student audience and teacher act as judges, or you could invite guest judges. Other students act as fact-checkers, either live or online depending on the ability of your students. What I love about this lesson is it encourages students to dig deeper when conducting research, as they want to find information that is unique and unknown. It also provides opportunities to discuss the validity of sources and media bias.

Objectives

Grades 4–12 students will be able to:

+ Conduct research to explore content standards on a deeper level.

+ Creatively present content for their intended audience.

+ Assess the credibility of information and sources.

Preparation

Materials:

+ Presentation program (Microsoft PowerPoint, Google Slides, Keynote, Buncee, or similar)

Instructions

 Consult the complete episode list of *Tell Me Something I Don't Know* (**tmsidk.com**), and choose one that is most relevant to share with your class. Because this podcast is intended for adults, you will need to preview the content to make sure it is appropriate. For younger classes, share a short clip from the show. Play one episode of the podcast with older students. Provide students a rubric and inform them that their presentations will be judged by the three key criteria: Is it true? Is it interesting? Is it something I didn't know?

 Divide students into groups of two to four and assign topics based on your content standards. You could also provide a list of topics and allow groups to choose. Provide time for students to conduct research and prepare their presentations. You may want to provide some instructional tutorials in finding valid sources, as well as how to fact-check information. Use the Show Me strategy to determine how much more time each group needs to finish conducting their research.

Set the stage for your presentations. Have fun with turning your classroom into a game show. You can add music and lights to get your students excited. You have some options for the actual presentations: You can allow students to fact-check during the presentation or provide them 5–10 minutes between each presentation.

Students can present their fact-checking challenges live or submit them to you through a form or online discussion. Students can also submit their choices for the winner through a form. I recommend keeping this fun and light-hearted. Inform students that winning or losing will not determine their grade. You could create a fun, unique trophy to display for the winning team or another fun award.

Extensions

Invite guest speakers to be judges. These can be school administrators or community members who work in a related field.

ONLINE AND REMOTE LEARNING ADAPTATION

Post a topic in the LMS and allow students to research and create a short presentation. Students upload presentations to the LMS, while other students view the presentations and offer feedback. Students fact-check and challenge any presentations with issues, and students vote for the presentation they feel best meets the criteria.

LESSON PLAN 6.3 **Character Debates Project**

Subject: Social Studies/ELA

Target Grades: 3–12

Duration: 2–3 class periods

Students assume the role of a historical character and conduct research to learn more about them. The teacher poses a question in an LMS discussion, and students respond to the question as they feel their character would. Students have opportunities to debate the other characters about the topic, helping them learn about opposing viewpoints of historical events and time periods.

Objectives

Grades 3–12 students will be able to:

✦ Apply their knowledge of historical events and characters to a class discussion.

✦ Create multimedia content to express the thoughts and opinions of the character they are assuming.

Standards Implemented in Lesson 6.3

ISTE STANDARDS FOR EDUCATORS	ISTE STANDARDS FOR STUDENTS	CONTENT AREA STANDARDS
Citizen 3b, 3c Designer 5b Facilitator 6a	Digital Citizen 2b, 2c Knowledge Constructor 3a, 3b, 3c, 3d Creative Communicator 6a, 6d	Students conduct ELA research to learn more about individuals from history and their actions, opinions, and viewpoints. Students develop a deeper understanding of historical time periods and events through a class discussion/debate.

Preparation

Materials:

+ ChatterPix Kids app or similar "talking character" app

+ LMS discussion board or another similar tool such as Padlet

+ To Do List Template (**bit.ly/to-dotasks**)

+ Optional: Paper and markers

Advanced Preparation:

+ Research historical events and useful context for the targeted time period.

+ Create questions that will spark a debate and elicit differing responses depending on the historical character.

Instructions

 Ask students to participate in a "brain dump" for 1–2 minutes to share what they learned about the time period or event you are discussing. For example, if you are discussing Ancient Egypt, students list everything they learned about this time period.

 Assign a historical figure to students, or allow them to select one from the time period you are studying. You can divide students into teams of two or three and assign them one character to portray together. This might make the debate/discussion a little more manageable. Another option is to provide a generic name to students with a set of characteristics, rather than a famous historical figure. For example, if you are studying World War II, you could assign a woman working in a factory, a soldier at war, and so on.

Provide students time to conduct preliminary research and create talking points for their character. Provide the To Do Task Template so students can divide responsibilities and track their progress using an online document.

Provide students the first question they will debate as their characters. For example, if you are studying colonial America, ask, "Should we colonize the New World? Why or why not?" Provide students time to research more about their historical figure.

Students can draw a picture of their character or find a copyright-friendly picture to use. Students use the ChatterPix Kids app (or similar) to make their character talk and respond to the question. ChatterPix Kids allows recordings of up to only 30 seconds, so students will need to be concise in their statements.

Students continue debating back and forth until you feel like they have discussed that question extensively. You could pose another question if needed.

Extensions

Invite a historian to view the presentations and provide feedback about any inaccurate information presented, as well as corroborating any good points made by students. This individual can also provide additional information related to the question.

ONLINE AND REMOTE LEARNING ADAPTATION

Explain the project in a videoconference call or post directions in an LMS assignment. Students research their character and create talking points. Students participate in an LMS discussion/debate, using ChatterPix Kids or a similar tool to make their character talk. This continues throughout the debate.

COACH'S CONNECTION

As we wrap up this book, I feel it is important to help teachers become more reflective about the impact of their projects. This Coach's Connection focuses on helping teachers incorporate research into their teaching. Additionally, I included a section on helping teachers move toward independence when implementing projects. The ideas and projects in this book will require a team approach; however, we want teachers to feel confident initiating these lessons even when a coach is unavailable. In my own work, I often struggle with helping teachers move toward independence, so my hope is that these ideas and strategies will help you in your role as a coach, while helping me as well.

Help Teachers Facilitate Action Research

According to Spencer (2017), *action research* is a type of research in which the teacher asks a question to determine if a teaching strategy, tool, or lesson is effective. They test this question, implementing the strategy with students and collecting data along the way. If you have tried action research before, you may, like me, have found it to be a rewarding and meaningful experience but also something that took time and a lot of effort. This is why action research is the perfect project for coaches to engage in with teachers, helping them ease into the process.

Action research is also an effective way to demonstrate the effectiveness of a technology integration strategy or tool you are implementing. The Data-Driven Decision-Maker standard calls on coaches to "assist educators and leaders in securely collecting and analyzing student data" and "support educators to interpret qualitative and quantitative data to inform their decisions and support individual student learning" (ISTE Standards for Coaches, 6a and 6b, 2019). Action research is one way to implement these standards, without teachers feeling like you are there to evaluate them or analyze their data. Rather, you are working together to find or create strategies and project templates, and then using action research to determine their effectiveness.

Research Steps

To get started with action research, you can follow this process outlined by Spencer (2017):

1. Inquiry process. Create a question. Typically, this will stem from a problem or challenge the teacher faces with their students, for example, feeling that students lack motivation or engagement when writing. You could ask, "How can peer review help improve student motivation for writing?" Help the teacher develop a question that is specific and measurable.

2. Design process. Next, determine the research you will conduct to answer this question. Determine the types of data you will collect, how you will collect it, and how to ensure that this study is ethical and protects student privacy. Ask for permission from your school administrators and/or district, although this may not be necessary unless you plan to publish this research. Create any surveys and data collection forms needed during the research. This is a great opportunity for conducting mini-lessons on relevant tools (Microsoft Forms, Google Forms, Microsoft Excel, or Google Sheets) and their data collection features, such as conditional formatting.

3. Action process. The action process will involve a cycle of experimentation and data collection. Repeat this process as needed, tweaking your experiment as you determine more effective ways to implement your strategies. In this mixed-method research, you and the teacher will be collecting two main types of data: *Quantitative* data, such as rubric scores and surveys, can be analyzed in numeric terms such as amounts or percentages. *Qualitative* data encompasses all non-numeric forms of data that are relevant to your research, such as photographs, journals or observations that are recorded, student or parent interviews, and more. As a coach, you can assist with this data collection as the teacher conducts their lesson or project.

4. Analysis process. This step involves organizing the data in charts and graphs, compiling any relevant qualitative research, and searching for trends or patterns in your data. Begin writing your results in a concise and clear format. You may also uncover more questions during this process, which will lead to additional action research.

5. Publishing process. While your action research may not be formally published in a scholarly journal or educational magazine, you may choose to share data with school or district administrators, other teachers, or your PLN members. This is a great time to gather feedback, encourage others to engage in their own action research around this topic, and advocate for the strategies or tools you tested.

Avoid Common Research Errors

A few common mistakes or influences can affect research results. Including coaches in the research process will help provide a second set of eyes and ears to reduce some of these errors. Being aware of these common errors will also help avoid them and ensure that your data and conclusions are valid:

✦ Bias. Various types of bias can influence research. When educators create a new strategy, it is natural to feel optimistic and expect positive learning outcomes. It is important to examine our data collection methods, surveys, and results to eliminate as much bias as possible. *Confirmation* bias is the tendency we have as humans to notice things that confirm our thoughts and feelings about something. For example, if you feel like students who eat healthy lunches do better at math, you will notice each time a student excels in math after eating healthy. You may unconsciously ignore instances that do not align with this belief or rationalize by thinking other factors must have influenced their low performance.

✦ Confounding variables. Think of confounding variables as "other factors" that could influence results. For example, if you are performing research to determine how peer review can increase motivation for student writing, be careful that no other new variables or factors were introduced. If at the same time you began your research, you implemented a new writing curriculum or moved your writing block to a different time, then it would be difficult to determine whether peer review was the cause of the increase in student motivation. Removing all variables during action research is extremely difficult, but be mindful of not introducing *more* as you are coaching a teacher through this process. It is natural for coaches to suggest new strategies during lessons or for teachers to alter their lessons because we are in the room with them. Even the smallest changes could affect the validity of your research, so it's important to evaluate your lessons to ensure that no confounding variables are present.

✦ Novelty Effect. The Novelty Effect occurs when the results of research are skewed based on the newness or novelty of the strategy or tool being tested. Initially, students get excited and more engaged, which can lead to greater learning outcomes. Consider implementing your research for a longer period of time to help eliminate this possibility.

✦ Sample size and population errors. Remember, action research typically focuses on only your own student population; the results of your study might not translate to other classrooms or schools. Because the purpose of action research is to make changes in your own classroom with your own students, this most likely is not an issue. However, it is important to note that your results may not translate globally.

Overall, make action research manageable and productive for you and the teachers you support. Yearlong studies may not be feasible, so shorter research periods may work best for you. Additionally, you may find that either quantitative or qualitative research works better, rather than employing a mixed-method approach. Anything you can do to encourage teachers to reflect and take part in this process is a step in the right direction.

Help Teachers Move Toward Independence with Projects

The first thing most coaches do when looking at the current ISTE Standards for Coaches is reflect on which standards they do well and which ones they need to improve upon—I certainly do. The Connected Learner standard encourages coaches to "establish shared goals with educators, reflect on successes and continually improve coaching and teaching practice" (ISTE Standards for Coaches, 2c, 2019). When reading this goal and reflecting on my practice, I recognize that I need improvement with helping move teachers toward independence when implementing projects. So, the following sections will focus on helping you tackle this, while (hopefully) helping me improve as well.

Establish Shared Goals

Creating goals is an important step toward success in any venture. When working with teachers during coaching sessions, ask them about their goals for implementing technology in their classroom. Their answers will help you establish a game plan and determine what milestones will look like. I really love this idea to have everything written down; it sets a framework for the amount of coaching you will provide, so there will not be any surprises as you ask the teacher to begin doing more independently. I admit that when I feel myself interjecting too much or doing more than I should, it is often when we did not establish a game plan from the beginning. Here are some questions you can ask yourself if you feel you are going down this path as a coach:

+ *Does this teacher truly understand all the steps needed to create and implement this project?* If the answer is no, then you are doing too much. If you do not think the teacher would be capable of creating and implementing the project independently after your coaching sessions, then this might not be an appropriate project for that class. I have had this happen numerous times! We want each project to be the best it can be for the students so we take one lesson up a notch, and then another, until eventually only an edtech guru could facilitate the lesson. It is not our job as coaches to show what we can do, but rather to help teachers implement projects that best fit what they can achieve independently. Asking yourself this question throughout a project will help you stay focused on the end goal: establishing teacher independence with implementing projects.

+ *While implementing the project, is it truly a collaboration between you and the teacher, or are you center stage?* Again, if you find that you are doing most of the work and the students are asking you all the questions, rather than seeking out you and their teacher equally, then this is a time to refocus. In these instances, I recommend waiting to address the situation until the next time you meet with the teacher and then taking full responsibility for taking over the lesson. Let them know that next time, you will be there "just in case" you are needed, but will take more of a backseat. One way to ensure that this happens is to make observations and take notes during the next session. This helps take you out of the mix and establishes the teacher as the primary facilitator. It also provides an opportunity for you to give timely feedback.

+ *Do you notice improvements in the teacher's confidence and ability to integrate technology and projects in their classroom?* If the answer is no, then you need to make some changes and revisit the original goals you set with this teacher. It is not always easy being a coach and a colleague to teachers. There is a balance between how much we push and how much we support, and it is better to provide more support than not enough. So I am letting myself off the hook for the times when I feel inadequate as a coach, and you should too!

Reflect on Successes and Areas of Need

Setting goals can only take us so far; we need to assess our progress toward them. Schedule time for reflecting on goals and making changes as needed. I recommend setting these appointments in advance, possibly even the first time you meet to begin implementing a project. Otherwise, life gets in the way and we begin focusing on urgent or new tasks rather than following through on existing projects. Often, we get caught up in the next "cool" idea and might not finish the first one. This process of goal setting and reflecting will ensure that coaches and teachers stay focused on the original goal and plan. As you move into the next project or goal, be sure to recognize the accomplishments the teacher made to help them appreciate their progress. It is easy for teachers to look at others who make technology integration look easy and forget about their own improvements and achievements. It is our role as the coach to build confidence and help teachers continue to grow, without skipping important skills and steps.

Parting Thoughts

My hope is that you close this book eager to begin implementing some of these ideas in your own classroom. Although many lessons and strategies in each chapter are based on research, I tweaked and adapted them to meet the unique needs of my students and classroom situations. I encourage you to do this as well, using your instincts and creativity to make the projects your own and involving your students in the planning process as much as possible. I look forward to hearing about your upcoming learning adventures and encourage you to use the hashtag #AuthenticEdVentures to share the lessons you implemented and ways that you tweaked these projects to make them your own. If you have questions or ideas, please reach out to me on Twitter at @KristinCHarr.

EDTECH COACHES PROFESSIONAL LEARNING COURSE MODEL

Appendix A provides a link to a course model outline for coaches planning to use this book for professional learning with teachers in your school or district. Additionally, you'll find some tips for designing your own courses in the future. Scan the QR code to access the outline, or go to **bit.ly/3dS5W8E**.

APPENDIX B

PROJECT EXAMPLES

Appendix B provides a link to project examples for many of the lesson plans included in this book. Scan the QR code to access the examples, or go to **bit.ly/38LtavP**.

ADVENTURES IN AUTHENTIC LEARNING TOOLBOX

Scan the QR code below to access all the templates and lesson plan documents shared in this book in one convenient location. You can also find them by visiting **bit.ly/34aAkJZ**.

REFERENCES

Anderson, A. [Amanda Anderson]. (2015, August 19). *How to link another slide in Google Slides* [Video]. YouTube. **youtube.com/watch?v=vDFQNFwUb8A**

Barron, B. (2000). Achieving coordination in collaborative problem-solving groups. *The Journal of the Learning Sciences, 9*(4), 403–436.

Boud, D., Cohen, R., & Sampson, J. (Eds.). (2014). *Peer learning in higher education: Learning from and with each other.* Routledge.

Centre for the Study of Historical Consciousness. (2020). The Historical Thinking Project. **historicalthinking.ca**

CPALMS. (2020). *Standards.* CPALMS. **cpalms.org/Public/search/Standard**

Gallo, C. (2018) No Apple presenter speaks for longer than 10 minutes, and the reason is backed by neuroscience. *Inc.* **inc.com/carmine-gallo/apple-follows-this-10-minute -rule-to-keep-you-glued-to-product-presentations.html**

Goodyear, P., Jones, C., & Thompson, K. (2014). Computer-supported collaborative learning: Instructional approaches, group processes and educational designs. In J. M. Spector, M. D. Merrill, J. Elen, & M. J. Bishop (Eds.) *Handbook of research on educational communications and technology* (pp. 439–451). Springer.

Hare, R. L., & Dillon, R. (2016). *The space: A guide for educators.* EdTechTeam Press.

Hoadley, C. (2018). A short history of the learning sciences. In F. Fischer, C. E. Hmelo-Silver, S. R. Goldman, & P. Reimann (Eds.) *International handbook of the learning sciences* (pp. 11–23). Taylor and Francis.

Hoogendoorn, C. (2016, May 26). The benefits of peer review. *Writing Across the Curriculum, Openlab at CityTech.* **openlab.citytech.cuny.edu/writingacrossthecurriculum /2015/05/26/the-benefits-of-peer-review**

Hopkins, G. (2017) *Twenty-five great ideas for teaching current events.* Education World. **educationworld.com/a_lesson/lesson/lesson072.shtml - sthash.2VQ5VFs8.dpuf**

International Society for Technology in Education. (2019). *ISTE Standards for Coaches.* **iste.org/standards/for-coaches**

International Society for Technology in Education. (2017). *ISTE Standards for Educators.* **iste.org/standards/for-educators**

International Society for Technology in Education. (2016). *ISTE Standards for Students.* **iste.org/standards/for-students**

Koehler, M. J. (n.d.) *The TPACK Game.* Dr. Matthew J. Koehler. **matt-koehler.com/the-tpack-game**

Larmer, J. (2018, July 13). A tricky part of PBL: Writing a driving question. PBLWorks. **pblworks.org/blog/tricky-part-pbl-writing-driving-question**

Mayer, R. E. (2008). Applying the science of learning: Evidence-based principles for the design of multimedia instruction. *American psychologist, 63*(8), 760.

NYU Metro Center. (2020). Culturally responsive curriculum scorecard. Metropolitan Center for Research on Equity and the Transformation of Schools. **research.steinhardt .nyu.edu/metrocenter/resources/culturally-responsive-scorecard**

Ormrod, J.E. & Jones, B. (2018). *Essentials of educational psychology: Big ideas to guide effective teaching* (5th edition). Pearson Education.

PBLWorks. (2020). *Gold standard PBL: Essential project design elements.* PBLWorks. **pblworks.org/what-is-pbl/gold-standard-project-design**

Pink, D. (2020, January). *Leadership, innovation, and the surprising truth of human motivation* [Address]. Future Of Education Technology Conference (FETC), Miami, FL.

ReadWriteThink (2003). *Narrative PQP peer-review form.* ReadWriteThink. **readwritethink.org/files/resources/lesson_images/lesson122/pqp_narrative.pdf**

Schrock, K., (2018). The 5 W's of website evaluation. Kathy Schrock's Guide to Everything. **http://schrockguide.net/uploads/3/9/2/2/392267/5ws.pdf**

Schwartz, D. L., Tsang, J. M., & Blair, K. P. (2016). *The ABCs of how we learn: 26 scientifically proven approaches, how they work, and when to use them.* WW Norton & Company.

Shabani, K., Khatib, M., & Ebadi, S. (2010). Vygotsky's Zone of Proximal Development: Instructional implications and teachers' professional development. *English Language Teaching, 3*(4), 237–248.

Spence, C. (2019, May 15). Science class: Connecting scientists with teachers and students. Explore. **explore.research.ufl.edu/science-class.html**

Spencer, J. [John Spencer]. (2017, January 11). *What is action research* [Video]. YouTube. **youtube.com/watch?v=Ov3F3pdhNkk&t=4s**

Spinks, A., (2007). *Evaluating websites.* andyspinks.com. **andyspinks.com/evaluating-websites**

Steinborn, M. B., & Huestegge, L. (2016). A walk down the lane gives wings to your brain. Restorative benefits of rest breaks on cognition and self-control. *Applied Cognitive Psychology, 30*(5), 795–805.

Sundar, K. (2020, June). *Guest post: Cut it out: Learning with seductive details.* The Learning Scientists. **learningscientists.org/blog/2019/6/20-1**

Thompson Earth Systems Institute. (2019). *Scientist in every Florida school.* Florida Museum. **floridamuseum.ufl.edu/earth-systems/scientist-in-every-florida-school**

US Department of Education. (2017, October). Early learning technology policy brief. **tech.ed.gov/files/2016/10/Early-Learning-Tech-Policy-Brief.pdf**

Watson, John (2008) Blended learning. The convergence of online and face-to-face learning. NACOL.

Wisniewski, B., Zierer, K., & Hattie, J. (2020, January 22). The power of feedback revisited: A meta-analysis of educational feedback research. *Frontiers in Psychology, 10.* **doi.org/10.3389/fpsyg.2019.03087**

INDEX

NUMBERS

A

B

C